High-Performance Person

Principles and rules for how you can achieve what you think is impossible. Learn, from the secrets of the most successful people in the WORLD

Steve Meyer

Steve Meyer

© **Copyright 2022 - All rights reserved.**

The content contained within this book may not be reproduced, duplicated or transmitted without direct written permission from the author or the publisher.

Under no circumstances will any blame or legal responsibility be held against the publisher, or author, for any damages, reparation, or monetary loss due to the information contained within this book. Either directly or indirectly.

Legal Notice:

This book is copyright protected. This book is only for personal use. You cannot amend, distribute, sell, use, quote or paraphrase any part, or the content within this book, without the consent of the author or publisher.

Disclaimer Notice:

Please note the information contained within this document is for educational and entertainment purposes only. All effort has been executed to present accurate, up to date, and reliable, complete information. No warranties of any kind are declared or implied. Readers acknowledge that the author is not engaging in the rendering of legal, financial, medical or professional advice. The content within this book has been derived from various sources. Please consult a licensed professional before attempting any techniques outlined in this book.

By reading this document, the reader agrees that under no circumstances is the author responsible for any losses, direct or indirect, which are incurred as a result of the use of information contained within this document, including, but not limited to, — errors, omissions, or inaccuracies.

Steve Meyer

Download Your Free Gift

Before you go any further, why not pick up a gift from us to you?

GROWTH PRINCIPLES

If you're willing to learn and transform yourself in all the right areas,

then success is definitely for you.

So, to find out how you can do that, let's get reading.

Scan the barcode to get it before it expires!

Table of Contents

Introduction..7

Chapter 1: What is a High-Performance Person?....................10

Chapter 2: Rules For A High-Performance Person...................20

Chapter 3: Principles Of The High-Performance Person..........24

Chapter 4: The Laws Of Performance.....................................35

Chapter 5: The Laws Of Planning...52

Chapter 6: The Law of Results..59

Chapter 7: The Law Of Expectations......................................67

Chapter 8: Practicing the Art and Science of Goal Setting.......75

Chapter 9: How To Defeat Procrastination And Disappointment..83

Chapter 10: How to Increase Your Persuasiveness...................89

Chapter 11: Why You Should Learn The Principles And Rules Of A High-Performance Person; How To Learn The Art And Science Of Goal Setting..97

Chapter 12: Proper Living is the Key To High Performance.....100

Chapter 13: How To Get Motivated..108

Conclusion...123

Thank You!...125

Download Your Free Gift...126

Introduction

No doubt, many of us have experienced a time in our lives where everything that could go wrong went wrong. No matter how hard we tried, we could not keep our minds focused on the positive happenings around us. You may not realize it, however, thoughts have power.

Whenever we think something, either good or bad, we give life to those thoughts.

Our thoughts determine our behaviors and our behaviors determine our actions. In my many years of working in the mental health field, I have noticed many people become stuck in negative mental spaces. They say negative comments about themselves, their futures, their finances, their careers, and their family. They profess defeatist remarks such as, "I'll never be successful," "Debt is a part of life," "This class is so hard; I don't think I can pass it," or "I don't like my job, but there are no other choices out there." They fail to realize their thoughts attract what they don't want in their lives. Scientific evidence points out that you attract what you think about. Here is the key; think positive thoughts and speak words of affirmation and encouragement every day. Whatever you want to achieve in life you must first think it. It is impossible to attract positive outcomes when you are consumed by negative thoughts.

Therefore, if you want to see the type of success you will have in the future, take a moment and think about your current thoughts. I know from experience, if you transform your thinking, you will expand your life!

Even in our down moments, we must learn how to think our way up. I know this is far from easy. How could you possibly think positive thoughts when everything around you speaks a different language? Remember, faith is the foundation of success. Before you can achieve anything, you must first think and believe that you can achieve it. You must also develop healthy mental habits to sustain you during those tough times.

Being mentally healthy is vital to your overall success and your ability to complete your goals. Don't forget, you will become what you think. Think about the way you want to be in the future, not about your current challenges and obstacles. Rather than occupying negative thoughts, transform your thinking. Think about where you want to be and then start taking small steps until you reach that destination. Then, your attitude will change. You will start feeling confident and courageous. You will walk with a little more "pep" in your step, speak with a little more certainty, tackle challenges with faith instead of fear, and dance as if no one is watching. By changing your thoughts you will improve every aspect of your life and you will begin to see yourself in the light you were created to shine in.

Before we can travel any distance —whether it is physical or mental—we must first prepare ourselves. The first seven Mental Healthy habits in this book will focus on powerful ways to increase your "mental readiness." Since success is a mindset, it is important to utilize this time to get "set" mentally. Therefore, before you jump right into Habit #1, it is important that you are clear on the definitions of the words think, up, and mental habits because you will see them repeatedly throughout this book. According to Webster's Dictionary, think means to purpose, to intend, to form an opinion, or to reflect, meditate, or ponder upon something. Mental habits refer to the presence of positive characteristics and thoughts that occur over and over.

Chapter 1: What is a High-Performance Person?

"A person is not a commodity. A person has worth. Have a purpose in life."

- Harry Truman

Growth

To be successful in life, you have to continuously grow. Growing means continuously feeding your brain with information. Information can come from many resources such as books, videos, audios, and the like. This is why most successful people read more books than anyone else. To get information you need physical materials and people. To get information from material things you will need to be able to manage time, technology, and money. To get information from people you will need to be able to motivate, encourage, and empathize with people.

Information

There is no knowledge that is not power. Information comes in different forms, shapes, and different styles. You need to have the right information for you at that particular point in time. Your brain has different perspectives every second, this is because your brain gathers information literally every second through all your senses therefore the information that you received a second ago will be perceived differently if you get it a second later. This is why you have to continuously learn and grow. This also explains why there is no knowledge that is not power because irrelevant information can be relevant a second later after your perspective has changed.

Management skills

To be able to work with time, technology and money, you will need technical skills such as planning, organizing, designing, and resource control. These four skills are the key management skills. If you have excellent management skills you will be able to use your resources effectively and efficiently to such an extent that you get relevant information that will enable you to achieve success.

Leadership

To be able to motivate, encourage and empathize with people you will need soft skills such as communication, listening, integrity, teamwork, and more. This is also known as leadership skills. If you use your leadership skills effectively you will be able to get all the information that you want and that is relevant for success from people. A leader has to realize that people need to be motivated, they need to be encouraged and they need to be energized through health and wellbeing.

Money

Everybody in life needs a source of income. We need money to survive. We need money to buy food, shelter, and all the necessary things in life. Most importantly, we need money to buy information directly or indirectly. This is why most people in life get a job or start their own businesses. Getting a job, making money, and getting rich will be explained in detail below.

Technology

Technology is one of the biggest physical materials that can give human beings a huge competitive advantage to get information. This is why information technology is changing the world and this is why the fourth industrial revolution is in fact information technology. Technology that can get you closer to information is the technology worth keeping.

People

A mind is a very complex organ in a human being. A mind stores all the information that a human being has, and for you to be able to access that information the person has to be in the right emotional state. For a person to be in the right emotional state all their needs will need to be taken care of including health, energy and the need to be motivated.

Leadership

Emotional Intelligence, Management, Productivity, Information, Growth, Success, Wealth...

Leadership deals with people, Management deals with other resources

Leadership is the ability to make sure that everyone reaches their goals effectively and efficiently. Life is full of problems that make people deviate from their plans and fail to reach their goals. When problems come, leadership and management are needed. Leadership deals with people not the problem. Management deals with the problem and not the people. Leadership plays a huge role in keeping everyone focused, motivated and empowered to be productive. The aim of leadership is to make sure that everyone feels at peace. A leader should focus more on people's well-being and a manager should focus on solving technical problems.

Authority

Leadership is not about solving technical problems, that is a job for a manager. A job of a manager is to make sure that they eliminate every problem that causes stress in people's lives. A job of a leader is to make sure that people are at peace knowing that the manager is solving problems and delegating. This means that the leader will have to communicate the message that the problem is being solved, they will have to empathize with people, build trust and if the problem doesn't get solved then a leader will have to resolve the conflict that may arise. A manager should come up with a plan to solve a technical problem and delegate tasks. This means that you should know when to act as a leader and know when to act as a manager. If you confuse the two, you are doomed. Leadership and management are skills which mean they can be learned. Just read books.

Management and Leadership

Management and leadership are dependent on each other. Managers have to be able to lead and leaders should be able to manage. Leaders should lead meaning they should interact with people then when they are done, they should manage the problem at hand. Managers should manage the problem and then lead the people by interacting with them. Never manage people. Manage the problem and lead the people. Solving the problem is called management. Making people feel at peace is called leadership. You need both skills and you should know when to act as a manager and when to act as a leader.

Teach, Mentor, Coach and Delegate.

No one man can be available to solve all problems when things go wrong therefore leaders and managers need to be able to coach, mentor and motivate everyone so that they will be ready to step in and take control when things go south.

Core Value of Leadership

This is a long list of fine values such as honesty, confidence, respect, empathy, etc. You should make a list of core values you want to learn and you should prioritize on learning and mastering them. Strong core values are what makes good leader.

Negotiation

You must be able to do everything with fewer resources i.e. time, energy and money. One way to do this is to negotiate for a better deal on your resources. Since leadership deals with people, leaders have to learn how to negotiate. This can include buying your resources in bulk and negotiating for a better discount. It is important to remain ethical and honest. Don't abuse your power to negotiate and offer people less than what is right. All things in life are connected by energy, if you are being unethical you are releasing negative energy that will come back to you. That's a story for another day.

Building Relationships

Leaders must be able to keep in contact with everyone they are in contact with. Communication is the center of everything. Leaders must use all the tools available to be able to communicate effectively and efficiently with everyone and information technology is making this possible.

Core Values Of a Good Leader

- Integrity.
- Ability to delegate.
- Communication.
- Self-awareness.
- Gratitude.
- Agility.
- Influence.
- Empathy.
- Patience.

How To Be A Good Leader

- Practice personal growth.
- Be a good team player.
- Read every day.
- Provide vision.
- Improve organizational structure.
- Set clear communication protocols.
- Delegate.
- Learn conflict management strategies.
- Coaching, mentoring and teaching.
- Communicate honestly and openly.
- Encourage people to read.
- Develop a positive attitude.
- Set clear goals and expectations.
- Focus on results not the process.
- Build Self-Confidence.
- Answer questions.
- Show people exactly what you want them to do.
- Do not overwork people.
- Lead by example.

- Don't get angry, just repeat what you said.

How to be a good team player

- Share information (ask and answer questions).
- Focus on goals and results, not the process.
- Be fair, positive, and supportive.
- Appreciate the benefits of diversity.
- Learn leadership skills.
- Be organized.
- Set clear goals.
- Have strong core values.
- Support risk-taking and change.
- Set clear, defined roles for each team member.
- Encourage diverse thinking.
- Distribute the work evenly.
- Focus on what is right. Don't play favorites.

Essential teamwork skills

- Communication.
- Conflict resolution.
- Problem-solving.

- Listening.
- Critical thinking.
- Collaboration.
- Leadership.
- Negotiation.

How to Teach, Mentor and Coach.

- Encourage active learning.
- Give constructive feedback.
- Respect different talents and ways of learning.
- Listen well and understand.
- Be patient.
- Read a lot of books.
- Be nonjudgmental.
- Be open to different opinions.
- Give examples and perspective.
- Answer questions.
- Asking open-ended questions.
- Learn emotional intelligence.

Chapter 2: Rules For A High-Performance Person

"Our job is not to make history, but to make the future."

- Ronald Reagan

Responsibility!

Many individuals prefer to ignore it and act as if it doesn't exist. However, if you want to be one of the world's most successful people, you should reconsider.

The most responsible people are those who have achieved great success. They understand that things do not merely happen to them; they have drawn them to them.

They understand that everything that occurs today results from a decision they made in the past that has brought them to this point.

Few people develop the high-value habit of responsibility, and it is one of their secrets to success.

It may not be easy to hold yourself accountable for everything that occurs in your life, but a wonderful thing occurs if you do. You become more powerful because you realize that the actions, decisions, and ideas you put out into the world come back to you.

And you were the one who did everything. Do you accept responsibility for everything that occurs in your surrounding

It is a skill to be responsible. It's something you learn. There are, however, various methods for doing so. Your behaviors help to shape your personality.

For instance, you decide whether you want to be lazy or get up early every day, or whether you want to save money or spend it carelessly. It's about showing yourself that you can be, and that you are accountable in the first place.

Rule 1: Stop complaining

Complainers are typically those who complain excessively while doing nothing. They can say many things, but when it comes to actually doing something about a problem, they are completely immobile.

Alternatively, you may quit whining and take charge of your destiny. If you don't like how a task is being completed, try it yourself or seek advice from the individual who did it incorrectly.

Rule 2: Overcome procrastination

High-performing people are those who put forth a lot of effort. You must work hard to earn and prosper in every element of your life. As a result, you must be responsible. You will not succeed if you do not have it.

Stop delaying and you'll be on your way to the top in no time. Stop squandering your time.

The time you wasted surfing the web, going through social media, or lounging around doing nothing could have been better spent elsewhere.

For example, you may have read a book, taken a walk, or worked out. Furthermore, you may have completed that project on which you had fallen behind. Anything besides wasting time would be preferable.

Rule 3: Be consistent and stick to your schedule

Having a routine is beneficial. Routine denotes order, which suggests you're on the correct course. For example, if you work, make an effort to get up at the same time every day.

Even on weekends, rather than remaining in bed until noon, you could get up early. It will help you maintain a level of consistency.

Plus, getting up early gives you extra time to do whatever tasks you had planned for the day.

Alternatively, you may unwind and enjoy your day off. If you are a student, you should develop the habit of studying regularly.

Alternatively, if you live abroad, remember to phone your friends and family at least once a week.

High-Performance Person

You should also develop a schedule for your professional and personal responsibilities. Keep a few things the same throughout the week if they are.

Getting off schedule can throw your entire routine off and throw you off balance.

Being responsible implies that you have complete control over your actions. You don't pass the buck to others, and you don't forget about your friends and family.

You should also avoid allowing laziness to dictate how you approach your work. If you're assigned a mission, you'll be able to complete it.

High-performing people behave in this manner. But, more significantly, they accept any responsibilities thrown at them, whether at work or in their personal lives.

They don't leave things half-finished or play the victim. Instead, responsible people take a solid stand on the ground; both feet planted firmly.

Chapter 3: Principles Of The High-Performance Person

"I am not a product of my circumstances. I am a product of my decisions."

- Stephen Covey

As you read this book, try to stand apart from yourself. Try to project your consciousness upward into a corner of the room and see yourself, in your mind's eye, reading. Can you look at yourself almost as though you were someone else?

Now try something else. Think about the mood you are now in. Can you identify it? What are you feeling? How would you describe your present mental state?

Now think for a minute about how your mind is working. Is it quick and alert? Do you sense that you are torn between doing this mental exercise and evaluating the point to be made out of it?

Your ability to do what you just did is uniquely human. Animals do not possess this ability. We call it "self-awareness" or the ability to think about your very thought process. This is the reason why man has dominion over all things in the world and why he can make significant advances from generation to generation.

This is why we can evaluate and learn from others' experiences as well as our own. This is also why we can make and break our habits.

We are not our feelings. We are not our moods. We are not even our thoughts. The very fact that we can think about these things separates us from them and from the animal world. Self-awareness enables us to stand apart and examine even the way we "see" ourselves—our self-paradigm, the most fundamental paradigm of effectiveness. It affects not only our attitudes and behaviors, but also how we see other people. It becomes our map of the basic nature of mankind.

In fact, until we take how we see ourselves (and how we see others) into account, we will be unable to understand how others see and feel about themselves and their world. Unaware, we will project our intentions on their behavior and call ourselves objective.

This significantly limits our personal potential and our ability to relate to others as well. But because of the unique human capacity of self-awareness, we can examine our paradigms to determine whether they are reality- or principle-based or if they are a function of conditioning and conditions.

The Social Mirror

If the only vision we have of ourselves comes from the social mirror—from the current social paradigm and from the opinions, perceptions, and paradigms of the people around us—our view of ourselves is like the reflection in the crazy mirror room at the carnival.

"You're never on time."

"Why can't you ever keep things in order?"

"You must be an artist!"

"You eat like a horse!"

"I can't believe you won!"

"This is so simple. Why can't you understand?"

These visions are disjointed and out of proportion. They are often more projections than reflections, projecting the concerns and character weaknesses of people giving the input rather than accurately reflecting what we are.

The reflection of the current social paradigm tells us we are largely determined by conditioning and conditions. While we have acknowledged the tremendous power of conditioning in our lives, to say that we are determined by it, that we have no control over that influence, creates quite a different map.

There are actually three social maps—three theories of determinism widely accepted, independently or in combination, to explain the nature of man. Genetic determinism basically says your grandparents did it to you. That's why you have such a temper. Your grandparents had short tempers and it's in your DNA. It just goes through the generations and you inherited it. In addition, you're Irish, and that's the nature of Irish people.

Psychic determinism basically says your parents did it to you. Your upbringing, your childhood experience essentially laid out your personal tendencies and your character structure. That's why you're afraid to be in front of a group. It's the way your parents brought you up. You feel terribly guilty if you make a mistake because you "remember" deep inside the emotional scripting when you were very vulnerable and tender and dependent. You "remember" the emotional punishment, the rejection, the comparison with somebody else when you didn't perform as well as expected.

Environmental determinism basically says your boss is doing it to you—or your spouse, or that bratty teenager, or your economic situation, or national policies. Someone or something in your environment is responsible for your situation.

Each of these maps is based on the stimulus/response theory we most often think of in connection with Pavlov's experiments with dogs. The basic idea is that we are conditioned to respond in a particular way to a particular stimulus.

How accurately and functionally do these deterministic maps describe the territory? How clearly do these mirrors reflect the true nature of man? Do they become self-fulfilling prophecies? Are they based on principles we can validate within ourselves?

Between Stimulus and Response

In answer to those questions, let me share with you the catalytic story of Victor Frankl.

Frankl was a determinist raised in the tradition of Freudian psychology, which postulates that whatever happens to you as a child shapes your character and personality and basically governs your whole life. The limits and parameters of your life are set, and, basically, you can't do much about it.

Frankl was also a psychiatrist and a Jew. He was imprisoned in the death camps of Nazi Germany, where he experienced things that were so repugnant to our sense of decency that we shudder to even repeat them.

His parents, his brother, and his wife died in the camps or were sent to the gas ovens. Except for his sister, his entire family perished. Frankl himself suffered torture and innumerable indignities, never knowing from one moment to the next if his path would lead to the ovens or if he would be among the "saved" who would remove the bodies or shovel out the ashes of those so fated.

One day, naked and alone in a small room, he began to become aware of what he later called "the last of the human freedoms"—the freedom his Nazi captors could not take away. They could control his entire environment, they could do what they wanted to his body, but Victor Frankl himself was a self-aware being who could look as an observer at his very involvement. His basic identity was intact. He could decide within himself how all of this was going to affect him. Between what happened to him, or the stimulus, and his response to it, was his freedom or power to choose that response.

High-Performance Person

In the midst of his experiences, Frankl would project himself into different circumstances, such as lecturing to his students after his release from the death camps. He would describe himself in the classroom, in his mind's eye, and give his students the lessons he was learning during his very torture.

Through a series of such disciplines—mental, emotional, and moral, principally using memory and imagination—he exercised his small, embryonic freedom until it grew larger and larger, until he had more freedom than his Nazi captors. They had more liberty, more options to choose from in their environment; but he had more freedom, more internal power to exercise his options. He became an inspiration to those around him, even to some of the guards. He helped others find meaning in their suffering and dignity in their prison existence.

In the midst of the most degrading circumstances imaginable, Frankl used the human endowment of self-awareness to discover a fundamental principle about the nature of man: Between stimulus and response, man has the freedom to choose.

Within the freedom to choose are those endowments that make us uniquely human. In addition to self-awareness, we have imagination—the ability to create in our minds beyond our present reality. We have conscience—a deep inner awareness of right and wrong, of the principles that govern our behavior, and a sense of the degree to which our thoughts and actions are in harmony with them. And we have independent will—the ability to act based on our self-awareness, free of all other influences.

Even the most intelligent animals have none of these endowments. To use a computer metaphor, they are programmed by instinct and/or training. They can be trained to be responsible, but they can't take responsibility for that training; in other words, they can't direct it. They can't change the programming. They're not even aware of it.

But because of our unique human endowments, we can write new programs for ourselves totally apart from our instincts and training. This is why an animal's capacity is relatively limited and man's is unlimited. But if we live like animals, out of our own instincts and conditioning and conditions, out of our collective memory, we too will be limited.

The deterministic paradigm comes primarily from the study of animals—rats, monkeys, pigeons, dogs—and neurotic and psychotic people. While this may meet certain criteria of some researchers because it seems measurable and predictable, the history of mankind and our own self-awareness tell us that this map doesn't describe the territory at all!

Our unique human endowments lift us above the animal world. The extent to which we exercise and develop these endowments empowers us to fulfill our uniquely human potential. Between stimulus and response is our greatest power—the freedom to choose.

"Proactivity" Defined

In discovering the basic principle of the nature of man, Frankl described an accurate self-map from which he began to develop the first and most basic habit of a highly effective person in any environment, the habit of proactivity.

While the word proactivity is now fairly common in management literature, it is a word you won't find in most dictionaries. It means more than merely taking initiative. It means that as human beings, we are responsible for our own lives. Our behavior is a function of our decisions, not our conditions. We can subordinate feelings to values. We have the initiative and the responsibility to make things happen.

Look at the word responsibility—"response-ability"—the ability to choose your response. Highly proactive people recognize that responsibility. They do not blame circumstances, conditions, or conditioning for their behavior. Their behavior is a product of their own conscious choice, based on values, rather than a product of their conditions, based on feeling.

Because we are, by nature, proactive, if our lives are a function of conditioning and conditions, it is because we have, by conscious decision or by default, chosen to empower those things to control us.

In making such a choice, we become reactive. Reactive people are often affected by their physical environment. If the weather is good, they feel good. If it isn't, it affects their attitude and their performance. Proactive people can carry their own weather with them. Whether it rains or shines makes no difference to them. They are value driven; and if their value is to produce good quality work, it isn't a function of whether the weather is conducive to it or not.

Reactive people are also affected by their social environment, by the "social weather." When people treat them well, they feel well; when people don't, they become defensive or protective. Reactive people build their emotional lives around the behavior of others, empowering the weaknesses of other people to control them.

The ability to subordinate an impulse to a value is the essence of the proactive person. Reactive people are driven by feelings, by circumstances, by conditions, by their environment. Proactive people are driven by values—carefully thought about, selected and internalized values.

Proactive people are still influenced by external stimuli, whether physical, social, or psychological. But their response to the stimuli, conscious or unconscious, is a value-based choice or response.

Principles of success

- Educate yourself.
- Choose your career wisely.
- Invest for every five years.
- Pay off bad debt.

High-Performance Person

- Avoid lifestyle inflation.
- Marry the right person.
- Don't think about useless things.
- Plan before doing.
- Failure is an opportunity to learn.
- Learn financial literacy.
- Mind your own business.
- Use taxes to your advantage.
- Never stop learning.
- Opportunity is always there.
- Thought and action create success.
- Grow, don't compete.
- Guide your thoughts to think positive.
- Save money for opportunities.
- Live below your means.
- Track your expenses daily.
- Be in charge of your own life.
- Don't blame, take responsibility.
- Think big.
- Set SMART goals.
- Accept change.

- Master time management.
- Be around winners.
- Take care of your health.

Chapter 4: The Laws Of Performance

If you don't value your time, neither will others. Stop giving away your time and talents. Value what you know & start charging for it.

– *Kim Garst*

Many possess the desire to succeed, yet few have the burning desire to change. High performers are able to grab success because they have identified habits that guide them on their journey. Perception plays a large role in how high performers view the world. In any given situation, high performers seek the challenge and welcome changing their perception for success.

Successful performers might use their character to push for success. Character traits of these individuals include integrity, courage, temperance, and humility. These character traits might include things like humility, integrity, courage, and temperance. High performers have shifted that push from success beyond their character to a personality. These personality traits include behavior, attitude, and image. High performers are not necessarily interested in quick fixes, simply to save time. They believe quick fixes are simply

Band-Aids for a short-term solution to the challenge. With this in mind, they focus their teams on shifting their habits into solving the problem, not just fixing it.

High performers assert that they are in charge. They choose the script of their life. It is through self-awareness that they take responsibility and are proactive in their decisions. They foster the ability to examine their character and decide how to view situations and their personal character. This ability allows them to control just how effective they are. In simple terms, they see the value that being proactive has on effectiveness. This is a major difference between those who are reactive. You see, reactive people understand that there is a problem, but they do not seek out the problem. They wait for the problem to fulfill the prophecy then react. Whereas, proactive people seek out the problem. They use not just responsibility but "response-ability" to solve problems before they have to react.

High performers use an arrow out approach to these problems. Understanding that they gain strength from the positive energy they have within their circle of influence. The circle of influence is basically the things that you can do something about. Whereas the challenge or issue is the circle of concern. The arrows out approach allow the performer to push positivity and seek solutions. While the arrows in approach are more reactive, this puts the performer into a negative spiral, often feeling like the victim. Shifting thinking to solution thinking and proactivity is another way that high performers boost their processes. Let's go a little deeper into the concept of concern, influence, and control.

High-Performance Person

To best understand how high performers work though this concept developed by Stephen Covey. I like to use this diagram. Feel free to create your own as we go through the next bit. High performers use these circles to categorize their challenges. They start by working with their team or individually to draw a large circle on a sheet of paper. This circle will represent the circle of concern. Within that circle, they place sticky notes of all the areas of concern they have for a specific project. They include everything from how they feel to needs. Next, draw a smaller circle inside the middle of the large circle; this is the circle of control. These would be all the things they can actually control. They move the things that they can actually control from concern into control. Many will feel that there are items that are out of their control, and this causes stress and anxiety. So we draw another circle between concern and control, and we call that influence. This is where we question those things that we feel are out of our control and look at is there a way we can influence a different result. The goal is to move all the notes from concern to either control or influence. This often provides an opportunity for self-discovery and innovative solutions.

The circle of influence tool is one that high performers use consistently. They question all the things that they feel are a concern and work to develop ways that they can influence or control the situations. They also understand that there are some things outside their control and are left with simple awareness that they cannot affect them, but they find relief in acknowledgment of these situations.

The vision of the high performer is what guides them to decide the value. With this in mind, they begin each challenge with the end in mind. Understanding that it is easy to busy yourself. High performers evaluate the concept of business and understand if a task really matters. This is how they know to take steps that really matter and lead them in the right direction.

These high performers use self-awareness to shape their lives; they do not focus on the standard or default preferences of others. They are the makers of their lives. Additionally, they understand their center. This is the source of wisdom, guidance, security, and power. This center is a fundamental part of their life and determines motivation, actions, decisions, and even interpretation of events. High performers have many different centers. Some find their center in self by being secure in the contestant changing and shifting of view of the world, and how circumstances, events, or decisions affect them. Others may be a family-centered with a foundation in family acceptance and fulfilling the expectations of their family. Traditions and family models often guide Their actions.

Others may be pleasure centered. This is to say the center themselves on what gives them the greatest pleasure. They see the world in terms of what gives them the greatest amount of pleasure. These centers fundamentally guide their daily motivations, actions, and decisions. Additionally, high performers also approach their center with principle, aligning beliefs, and values with behaviors. This leads to high performers maintaining the exceptional discipline to focus on their challenges and goals. They have to have the willpower to do things even when they don't want to. They focus on acting in accordance with their values rather than impulse and desire.

The high performer often is an empathic listener. They seek to understand the challenge before offering a solution. In order to be effective in this way, they have to learn to listen. Yet it is more than just listening. An empathetic listener is an inspiring characteristic. It requires a fundamental shift in the paradigm. It means the individual no longer seeks to be understood, yet they listen with the intent to understand, not simply reply. As an empathetic listener, they evaluate what is said, then probe to ask questions for a frame of reference. Then give counsel to advise based on their personal experience. Finally, they try to figure out the motives or behavior based on their own motives. This gives high performers a deeper understanding of other's needs and increases their credibility.

They also understand that there is value in differences. The perspective of another person provides the opportunity to uncover possibilities that they may not have considered. Embracing this allows them to see value in differences and expand perspective. It also helps to remove negativity from potential preconceived notions and look for the good in others. As well, it enhances their courage and ability to be interdependent on others, encouraging them to be open. As they become more open, they open themselves to solutions that those with a closed perspective may not have even thought possible.

Additionally, high performers understand that they must devote time to renewing themself mentally, spiritually, physically, and socially. It is through this renewal that they can take all the concepts of the seven habits and increase performance. High performers are aware that there are four areas that each requires balance. Mentally they continuously expand their mind. They do this through reading, journaling, and using enriching programs. Spiritually they focus on their values with reinforcement of the commitment of the system at their core. This could be through meditation, prayer, being in nature, or reading. Physically they ensure to renew themself by sufficient rest, eating well, and building endurance. Lastly, they renew themselves socially by developing meaningful relationships. They seek to understand other people deeply. As they focus on renewing and working to embrace positivity. The

look to be an inspiration to others through empathy and by encouraging proactivity.

Habit 1 – Value in Time

High performers understand that not all uses of time are equal. This simple truth is part of what sets them apart from standard performers. Those performing at high levels spend their time focusing on more profitable work. They spend their time investing in people to build relationships. Creating flexible careers and enjoy more freedom. As well they typically contribute more to society. They have accomplished all this because they know how to manage time on a daily basis effectively.

High-Performance Person

High performers also understand their own value. They have an internal gauge for how much their time is worth. They have an intrinsic ability to know if a task is worth their time. At all levels of performance, people make choices to decide if things are worth their time. Even if it is as simple as do I pay a lawn service to cut the grass to save one hour of time. Is my time worth $40 to have the service? We all make choices like these every day. However, the majority of people base their decision on feelings or guesswork rather than actual calculations. High performers truly weigh out the value of what the hour is worth. If they can put that same hour of cutting the grass into personal development, closing a deal, or self-care then it may be worth the $40 to have the grass cut by someone else. Each person has to determine their own personal value.

High performers do not waste time focusing on things that are not in the scope of their vision. They focus on what they want and know the core values to achieve it. They also understand that the value of free time is non-negotiable. It is easy to begin calculating the value of your time and pushing yourself to work more hours. High performers understand that there cannot be a monetary value set to their free time. This time rewards them for the hours of work they have already done. These rewards can be anything from enjoying music to volunteering within the community. High performers that want to set a value for a free time give it a value based on the level of happiness or meaningfulness the task adds to their life.

Furthermore, they focus on the value of time management. This is one quality they take very seriously. This is because they understand that time is limited; there is a finite amount of time each day. So they work to ensure that they consistently use the time they have to the best of their abilities. They also understand that when they take control of their time, they improve their ability to focus and accomplish more with less time. Regardless of the method they use for blocking time or list-making, they quickly can see that they have greater momentum and improved decision-making abilities. High performers understand that without structure and a plan for their time, it is way too easy to just jump into decisions and not have time to assess the best option. By using effective time management, they are able to improve their decision-making skills and avoid stress in many situations. This is not to say that emergencies do not arise, but that they are better prepared in those situations because every decision is not a reaction. This allows them to be in greater control of their day and ultimately push towards achieving their vision.

Every Attempt a Learning Opportunity

Looking back over the last thousand years, from say the year 1,000 to the year 2,000, if we pick out the most influential figures, the men and women who shaped the course of history, we might choose Johannes Gutenberg who developed the printing press or Christopher Columbus or Galileo. Isaac Newton might be on our list or Martin Luther. These surely are men who shaped history. I want to introduce to you now someone who more than molded history. This individual influenced and continues to influence to this day virtually every aspect of your personal and professional life. This was the man who lit up the world and provided power to the masses.

Thomas Alva Edison is best known for his refinement of the electric light bulb and invention of the phonograph and the movie camera, but probably his most far reaching innovation was his process for generating and distributing electricity. Edison is the man who brought us light, where and when we need it.

The economical generation and distribution of electricity began the evolution of processes that regulate climate inside buildings, physically move people around the world and allow people to communicate instantaneously today. Edison's insights serve us like none other.

In his lifetime Edison secured some 1,093 patents in the United States alone. He held many more in Europe. He was a prolific inventor, a perceptive scientist and an accomplished business man. But, you might not have bet on his success had you known him as a child and young man.

Fortunately for all the people who have benefitted and will yet benefit from his genius Thomas Edison forged high performance habits from the beginning. These habits served him, and us, well.

Thomas was the youngest of seven children. As an infant he suffered a bout with scarlet fever that severely limited his ability to hear. Through his life, though he recognized this disability, he never let his hearing loss slow him down. He believed his deficiency hearing provided him a greater ability to think.

Thomas didn't learn to speak until he was four years old. Once he could communicate though he began to take the world by storm.

The epitome of an inquisitive youngster, Thomas peppered his parents with questions about everything. He wanted to know how things work and why. With a house full of children and other competing interests to attend to Thomas' parents channeled his energy and his voracious appetite for learning as best they could.

At the age of seven Thomas attempted to begin a formal classroom education. His teacher, trying to manage a single-room schoolhouse with 38 children determined Thomas was hyperactive and prone to distraction. Thomas' teacher labeled him "difficult." We might label him ADHD (attention deficit hyperactivity disorder) today. Of course our solution for ADHD is drugs. Back then support was the order of the day. When Thomas' mother Nancy Edison, a gifted teacher in her own right, realized school was not going well for Thomas she settled on a better route, home schooling, and got to work.

Edison's mother was the defining influence of his life. She nurtured him, encouraged him and directed him. She believed in him so much he couldn't help but believe in himself. Nancy focused Thomas' education on mastering reading, writing, and arithmetic with a solid grounding in the Bible. Thomas' father for his part encouraged the young student to read the classics.

High-Performance Person

Thomas was so enthralled by learning that when first introduced to a library he committed to start in one corner and systematically read every book on every shelf. His parents convinced him there was a better approach to learning and a more efficient use of his time and energy.

Thomas Edison had ambition and desire, but also recognized he possessed limitations. He developed a unique process of independent learning and self-education that carried him through a lifetime of scientific and industrial exploration and achievement.

Early on as he labored through the classics, like Newton's Principia, Edison was disillusioned by obscure, aristocratic language. He was enthralled however, by the pure genius of the concepts, the theories and the laws most clearly defined through mathematics. Edison recognized at an early age what wisdom he could glean from the lives and writings of great men and women, but he also internalized the fact that these writers could be caught in traps of self-deception and error. So he tested every relevant theory he came across to prove the concept for himself. His thoroughness and attention to detail helped him avoid those traps of self-deception as best he could.

Along with his habit of personal growth and development, and really as a means to further it, Edison cultivated nearly unwavering perseverance. He kept at a task, no matter how challenging until he had it figured out. This single trait put him in a class by himself. He was not to be one who stopped short of the finish line. What others termed as failures Edison saw as learning attempts. He didn't fail; he discovered ways things wouldn't work.

At the age of 12 Edison decided it was time; time to make his own way. He started selling newspapers and snacks on the local train. He built a business where he managed other boys doing the selling and he even started publishing and distributing his own newspaper. His publishing business was so profitable he was able to furnish an extensive laboratory to facilitate his experimentation. Everything didn't always go smoothly however. A makeshift lab Edison built on a rail baggage car set fire to the train. He lost access to the railroad.

A fortuitous event helped Edison secure a position as a telegraph operator. He positioned himself at the cutting edge of technology and became somewhat of a journeyman operator, traveling around the Midwest for five years pursuing opportunity while continuing to tinker. Upon stopping back to check in on his family he saw his parents were not doing well. He decided he had to buckle down and make things happen. On the advice of a friend, he took a permanent telegraph operator position with Western Union in Boston, Massachusetts, a hub for learning and the development of cutting edge technology.

While working 12-hour days, six days a week for Western Union Edison continued to experiment and tinker. His first patent was for an automated vote counting machine. After much effort he realized no one wanted his device. Motivated by this disheartening experience he resolved to focus on inventing things that could succeed in the marketplace; devices people would want to buy.

Edison's employers at Western Union were growing impatient with his moonlighting ventures which were distracting from his job performance. So Edison borrowed money from a friend and headed for the "Big Apple." After a few weeks in New York Edison was struggling not so much to succeed, but to survive. Then another fortuitous event reestablished him on his path.

After begging for money in the financial district Edison began wandering through buildings. He came across a financial services manager all in a tizzy. His stock ticker had stopped working and no one could figure it out. Having been sleeping in the basements of office buildings in the financial district Edison had already acquainted himself with these devices. He gave it a go and easily corrected the breakage. He was hired on the spot for a salary of $300 per month.

Seeing a need Edison went on to develop improvements to stock ticker technology and at the age of 22 sold the rights to these improvements for $40,000; a substantial sum at the time.

With this seed money Edison set up a small laboratory and manufacturing facility in Newark, New Jersey. He grew that laboratory into the first mass-production research facility in the world. Edison hired and allied himself with other creative ambitious men and went on to unparalleled achievements inventing, developing businesses and industrial processes, and advancing the industrial revolution.

Thomas Edison was a man with a big appetite for learning. From humble beginnings he built an industrial empire. He recognized his own shortcomings early on. Instead of letting his weaknesses slow him down he focused on his strengths and built on success. He vowed to not worry about things beyond his control. Perseverance and a willingness to go where others had not ventured set him apart from the masses. No attempt was wasted. Every attempt was a learning opportunity.

Thomas Edison adopted habits which always kept him moving forward. He became affectionately known as the Wizard of Menlo Park; an extraordinary success.

His high performance habits lit up our lives.

The Right Habits

Thomas Edison and Andrew Carnegie exhibited remarkably similar characteristics. They both used high performance habits to achieve phenomenal success. They both worked diligently on improving themselves; they were always learning. They had the habit of always going the extra mile; doing more than was required. They had the habit of being open to opportunity; they were willing to move forward and take measured risks. And they had the habit of networking; of building partnerships and deliberately associating with and surrounding themselves with exceptional people. These were the habits that made the "Prince of Steel" and the "Wizard of Menlo Park".

Super successful people either instinctively or consciously and deliberately choose, develop and nurture habits that allow them to move faster, travel farther and accomplish more than the average masses of the great unwashed. High achievers leverage the RIGHT HABITS; habits that make all the difference.

What about you?

Do any of these routines lay claim to your time, energy and talents?

- Watching television excessively (enough to interrupt other activities including sleep).
- Nail biting or playing with your hair.
- Constantly checking your smartphone or posting useless information to the net.
- Snacking compulsively or eating too much processed or fast food.
- Overspending or impulsively shopping.
- Smoking or drinking.
- Routinely interrupting other people when they speak.
- Avoiding eye contact.
- Peppering your speech with "um", "ah", "like", "you know" or expletives.

We're all familiar with bad habits. We recognize them in other people right away, but we rarely recognize them in ourselves. This list of "bad" habits is a selection of some of the most common habits people settle into.

Each of the habit routines is a process that begins with a cue stirring up a craving and ends with some level of satisfaction; a feeling reward. We employ habits to meet our needs; even needs that ultimately limit us, hold us back, and keep us from achieving our potential.

Many of the needs we satisfy by means of habit, particularly bad habits, those habits that don't serve us, are unconscious. We are not even aware we have these habits. Our core beliefs about the world, ourselves and our place in it have nurtured these habits.

We often opt for the comfort of the known over the discomfort of the unknown. We choose the cropped effort of a routine over the pain and discomfort required to exert ourselves to surge down a new path.

The bad habits I mentioned earlier are examples of observable habit cycles. They include observable physical routines.

More insidious and potentially more limiting are our habits of mind or thought habits. These are thinking loops that can significantly impact our lives and inhibit the expression of our vast potential.

We establish thought patterns to achieve the same ends as action habits. We unconsciously want to feel good or at least feel better about ourselves and we don't want to expend too much effort. Instead of exerting ourselves examining a new perspective we just adopt a mental shortcut; a habit of thought.

Habits of thought can stilt our thinking and draw in the boundaries of our minds. We in effect think ourselves into a box, all to make life easier. What we end up doing is make life worse.

Chapter 5: The Laws Of Planning

"Perfection is not when there is no more to add, but no more to take away."

- Antoine de Saint-Exupéry

Because that's how nature has made any human body to work, it is stated that rising early is right for you. Early to bed and early to increase, makes a person healthy, wealthy and smart" is an age-old stating told and retold the world over. There are some, still untouched by even the thought of increasing early.

Early rising is the practice of getting up at an extremely early time every morning, well before most other individuals are awake. A lot of early birds get up a long time around 5 am in the early morning, giving them a long continuous period when they can get essential work done, throughout the day when their energy and passion and determination are most significant. Early increasing is a fantastic practice to adopt, and I understand that the times in my life when I've gotten the most done were those times when I got up early every day like clockwork.

Early increasing isn't that tough of a habit to develop, and if you enjoy the advantages, then you'll have an even simpler time. When you wake up is not a curse at being up so early and complain about being tired, the first thing you require to do. When you wake up in the morning is welcome the day with thankfulness, the very first thing you should do. The Dalai Lama recommends he awaken and state "Today I am lucky to have woken up, I live, I have valuable human life, I am not going to squander it. I am going to utilize all my energies to develop myself, to broaden my heart out to others, to accomplish enlightenment for the benefit of all beings, I am going to have kind thoughts towards others, I am not going to get angry or think severely about others, I will be as beneficial to others as I can.

Habit Or Natural Predisposition

I had heard good friends say they are night owls and don't do early mornings while others are up and have completed half a day's work before the likes of me rolled out of bed. I challenged myself to alter this habit; however, just in the last two years after I realized how much I might achieve in my life by increasing earlier.

Relationship between Rising Early and Productivity

Anybody who has followed or check out the practices of successful people would instantly see that there is a connection between increasing early and their productivity/success. I work from home and so when I hear footsteps of passers-by who are going to work, I am already halfway through my to-do-list I usually set the night before.

Ways to start rising early

Were people born or made in the morning? I seldom went to bed around nighttime in my middle 20s and always slept late all the time.

After a while, I couldn't neglect the great connection between success and increasing early, even in my own life. On those uncommon occasions where I did get up soon, I noticed that my efficiency was often greater, not just in the morning however throughout the day. And I likewise saw a significant feeling of wellness. Being the proactive goal-achiever, I was, I set out to end up being a habitual early riser. I promptly set my alarm clock for 5 AM...

... And the next early morning, I got up just before midday.

I figured I need to have been born without the early riser gene. When I applied those ideas, I was able to end up being an early riser consistently.

It's challenging to end up being an early bird using the wrong strategy. But with the right approach, it's relatively simple.

The most common wrong strategy is this: You assume that if you're going to get up previously, you'd better go to bed earlier. If you now sleep from midnight to 8 am, you figure you'll go to bed at 10 pm and get up at 6 am instead.

It seems there are two primary schools of thought of sleep patterns. One is that you ought to go to sleep and get up at the same time every day. It's like having an alarm clock on both ends-- you try to sleep the same hours each night. This appears useful for residing in contemporary society. We need predictability in our schedules. And we need to ensure adequate rest.

The 2nd school says you ought to listen to your body's requirements and go to bed when you're worn out and get up when you naturally get up. This approach is rooted in biology. Our bodies need to know how much rest we require, so we ought to listen to them.

Through trial and error, I learned for myself that both schools are suboptimal sleep patterns. Both are wrong if you care about productivity. Here's why:

If you sleep set hours, you'll sometimes go to sleep when you aren't tired enough. You aren't tired enough if it's taking you more than 5 minutes to fall asleep each night. You're losing time depending on bed awake and not being asleep. Another issue is that you're presuming you need the same number of hours of sleep every night, which is a false assumption. Your sleep requires differing from day to day.

If you sleep based on what your body tells you, you'll probably be sleeping more than you need-- in numerous cases a lot more, like 10-15 hours more per week (the equivalent of a full waking day). Most sleepers get 8 + hours every night, which is typically too much.

When I was awake (and only when I was asleep), I had the choice to go to bed and get up with my alarm clock at a fixed time (7 days per week). I wake up all the time at the same time (in my case at 5 am), but at different times, I go to bed every night.

I sleep many times in 3 minutes when I go to bed. Sometimes I go to bed at 9:30 pm; others live before midnight. I go to bed for several nights between 10 and 11 pm.

The longer I wake up, the more likely I am to return to sleep. I figure out. I found out. But if I want to sleep in, I wake up all the time.

After a couple of days, I found that my sleep patterns had become a natural rhythm. I would be resting early and sleeping the next night if I had been sleeping too little for one night. And if I had so much time if I weren't exhausted, I'd sleep less. The body chose to kill me as it realized that I would stand up always immediately and the wake-up time could not be controlled.

A later result was that I slept about 90 minutes less per night on average, but I felt better. I slept almost the whole time I was in bed.

So, you want your day to get early (or have more control of your sleep patterns), then think of it: go to bed if you are too tired to keep awake and get up at some point and morning.

The Habit Of Self-Investment

The best investment anybody can make, if not the only one that will make the straightest effect in your life, is to buy yourself. This is crucial to success if you desire to achieve any goal in your life, anything, profession, or service concerning your life. Too many individuals buy a lot of other things but continuously forget to buy themselves which supports the premise that there are just a few who are content in their lives.

If you think you understand everything, it means you are in a world of trouble. Nobody understands everything, however, what you know you require applying it in your life properly.

Investing in yourself means you have acknowledged there is more to discover. In the details age, we need to know how to manipulate the information we receive, and because it comes at us so frequently, we require being open-minded.

Possibly you want to purchase real estate or stocks and bonds, a brief course, online academic learning system or a live seminar will do the technique for you. Today we can gain from the comfort of our house, on the web, CD, DVD or internet radio.

Winners in life often read, compose often and share their understanding with others. I delight in discovering older people who always wanted to earn their high school diploma and age the age of 70 or 80 they finish from high school.

Investing in yourself is the best financial investment you can make.

The factor for this is when you invest in yourself; you are increasing your true personal worth. When you make investments in savings debentures, bonds, stocks, property or anything else that may give you are return on your cash, you may be increasing your financial worth; however, this does not always imply you are growing your true individual worth.

Your true individual worth transcends your financial value, merely the same as an individual who finds out how to fish is worth more than the fish that are captured. The values are different. Because one chicken is worth numerous eggs.

Buying yourself is how you create real individual wealth, because, even if you were to lose all your product wealth, you would still know to overcome your adversity, survive, and prosper once again.

Among the problems that happen when people acquire material wealth, without having to find out how to obtain it, is if they tend to lose it; this is since they were not rich and poor at all, and they will most likely remain bad unless they acquire the knowledge of how to be abundant. If you do not understand how to do something, you need to discover, and if you have not learned what to do, then you will not be able to do whatever it is that you require doing. When it comes to collecting material wealth, you need discovering how to do it, just in case somebody takes it far from you. And, never believe that you cannot lose the wealth you have because individuals who are more than likely to lose wealth are the ones who did not make it or find out how to acquire it and after that keep it.

If you have genuinely invested in yourself, you will overcome your scenarios and bounce back very rapidly. When you have discovered how to do something like collect wealth and comprehend the concepts required, then you will find your real worth.

Chapter 6: The Law of Results

"To get the results you want, you have to get the details right."

- Jack Welch

The concept of maximizing performance by alternating periods of activity with periods of rest was first advanced by Flavius Philo-stratus (A.D. 170–245), who wrote training manuals for Greek athletes. Russian sports scientists resurrected the concept in the 1960s and began applying it with stunning success to their Olympic athletes. Today, "work-rest" ratios lie at the heart of periodization, a training method used by elite athletes throughout the world.

The science of periodization has become more precise and more sophisticated over the years, but the basic concept hasn't changed since it was first advanced nearly two thousand years ago. Following a period of activity, the body must replenish fundamental biochemical sources of energy. This is called "compensation" and when it occurs, energy expended is recovered. Increase the intensity of the training or the performance demand, and it is necessary to commensurately increase the amount of energy renewal. Fail to do so and the athlete will experience a measurable deterioration in performance.

Energy is simply the capacity to do work. Our most fundamental need as human beings is to spend and recover energy.

We need energy to perform, and recovery is more than the absence of work. It serves not just health and happiness, but also performance. Nearly every elite athlete we have worked with over the years has come to us with performance problems that could be traced to an imbalance between the expenditure and the recovery of energy. They were either overtraining or undertraining in one or more dimensions—physically, emotionally, mentally or spiritually. Both overtraining and undertraining have performance consequences that include persistent injuries and sickness, anxiety, negativity and anger, difficulty concentrating, and loss of passion. We achieved our breakthroughs with athletes by helping them to more skillfully manage energy—pushing themselves to systematically increase capacity in whatever dimension it was insufficient, but also to build in regular recovery as part of their training regimens.

Balancing stress and recovery is critical not just in competitive sports, but also in managing energy in all facets of our lives. When we expend energy, we draw down our reservoir. When we recover energy, we fill it back up. Too much energy expenditure without sufficient recovery eventually leads to burnout and breakdown. (Overuse it and lose it.) Too much recovery without sufficient stress leads to atrophy and weakness. (Use it or lose it.) Just think about an arm placed in a cast for an extended period of time in order to protect it from the "stress" to which it is ordinarily subjected. In a very short time, the muscles of the arm begin to atrophy from disuse. The benefits of a sustained fitness program decrease significantly after just one week of inactivity—and disappear altogether in as few as four weeks.

The same process occurs emotionally, mentally and spiritually. Emotional depth and resilience depend on active engagement with others and with our own feelings. Mental acuity diminishes in the absence of ongoing intellectual challenge. Spiritual energy capacity depends on regularly revisiting our deepest values and holding ourselves accountable in our behavior. Full engagement requires cultivating a dynamic balance between the expenditure of energy (stress) and the renewal of energy (recovery) in all dimensions.

We call this rhythmic wave oscillation, and it represents the fundamental pulse of life.

The more powerful our pulse, the more fully engaged we can be. The same is true organizationally. To the degree that leaders and managers build cultures around continuous work—whether that means several-hour meetings, or long days, or the expectation that people will work in the evenings and on weekends—performance is necessarily compromised over time. Cultures that encourage people to seek intermittent renewal not only inspire greater commitment, but also more productivity.

Instead, most of us tend to live far more linear lives. We assume that we can spend energy indefinitely in some dimensions—often the mental and emotional—and that we can perform effectively without investing much energy at all in others—most commonly the physical and the spiritual. We become flat liners.

Nature itself has a pulse, a rhythmic, wavelike movement between activity and rest. Think about the ebb and flow of the tides, the movement between seasons, and the daily rising and setting of the sun. Likewise, all organisms follow life-sustaining rhythms—birds migrating, bears hibernating, squirrels gathering nuts, and fish spawning, all of them at predictable intervals.

So, too, human beings are guided by rhythms—both those dictated by nature and those encoded in our genes. Seasonal affective disorder (SAD) is an illness that is attributable both to changes in seasonal rhythms and to the body's inability to adapt. Our breathing, brain waves, body temperature, heart rates, hormone levels and blood pressure all have healthy (and unhealthy) rhythmic patterns.

We are oscillatory beings in an oscillatory universe. Rhythmicity is our inheritance.

Oscillation occurs even at the most basic levels of our being. Healthy patterns of activity and rest lie at the heart of our capacity for full engagement, maximum performance and sustained health. Linearity, by contrast, ultimately leads to dysfunction and death. Just picture for a moment the undulating wave form of a healthy EEG or EKG—and then think about the implications of their opposite: a flat line.

At the broadest level, our activity and rest patterns are tied to circadian rhythms (circa dies, "around a day"), which cycle approximately every twenty-four hours. In the early 1950s, researchers Eugene Aserinsky and Nathan Kleitman discovered that sleep occurs in smaller cycles of 90- to 120-minute segments. We move from light sleep, when brain activity is intense and dreaming occurs, to deeper sleep, when the brain is more quiescent and the deepest restoration takes place. This rhythm is called the "basic rest-activity cycle" (BRAC). In the 1970s, further research showed that a version of the same 90-to 120-minute cycles—ultradian rhythms (ultra dies, "many times a day")—operates in our waking lives.

These ultradian rhythms help to account for the ebb and flow of our energy throughout the day. Physiological measures such as heart rate, hormonal levels, muscle tension and brain-wave activity all increase during the first part of the cycle—and so does alertness. After an hour or so, these measures start to decline. Somewhere between 90 and 120 minutes, the body begins to crave a period of rest and recovery. Signals include a desire to yawn and stretch, hunger pangs, increased tension, difficulty concentrating, an inclination to procrastinate or fantasize, and a higher incidence of mistakes. We are capable of overriding these natural cycles, but only by summoning the fight-or-flight response and flooding our bodies with stress hormones that are designed to help us handle emergencies.

The long-term cost is that toxins build up inside us. We can only push so hard for so long without breaking down and burning out. Stress hormones that circulate chronically in our bodies may be temporarily energizing, but over time they prompt symptoms such as hyperactivity, aggressiveness, impatience, irritability, anger, self-absorption and insensitivity to others. Override the need for oscillation long enough and the symptoms may extend to headaches, back pain, gastrointestinal disorders, and ultimately to heart attacks and even death.

Because the body craves oscillation, we will often turn to artificial means to make waves when our lives become too linear. When we lack sufficient energy to meet the demands in our lives, for example, we turn to stimulants such as caffeine, cocaine and amphetamines. When we can't relax naturally, we may begin to rely on alcohol, marijuana and sleeping pills to cool down. If you are drinking several cups of coffee to stay alert during the day and a couple of drinks or several glasses of wine to disengage in the evening, you are simply masking your own linearity.

To live like a sprinter is to break life down into a series of manageable intervals consistent with our own physiological needs and with the periodic rhythms of nature. This insight first crystallized for Jim when he was working with world-class tennis players. As a performance psychologist, his goal was to understand the factors that set apart the greatest competitors in the world from the rest of the pack. Jim spent hundreds of hours watching top players and studying tapes of their matches. To his growing

High-Performance Person

frustration, he could detect almost no significant differences in their competitive habits during points. It was only when he began to notice what they did between points that he suddenly saw a difference. While most of them were not aware of it, the best players had each built almost exactly the same set of routines between points. These included the way they walked back to the baseline after a point; how they held their heads and shoulders; where they focused their eyes; the pattern of their breathing; and even the way they talked to themselves.

It dawned on Jim that these players were instinctively using the time between points to maximize their recovery. Many lower-ranked competitors, he began to see, had no recovery routines at all. When he hooked up the top players to EKG telemetry, which allowed him to monitor their heart rates, he made another startling discovery. In the sixteen to twenty seconds between points in a match, the heart rates of top competitors dropped as much as twenty beats per minute. By building highly efficient and focused recovery routines, these players had found a way to derive extraordinary energy renewal in a very short period of time. Because lesser competitors had no comparable routines between points, their heart rates often remained at high levels throughout their matches regardless of their level of fitness. The best competitors were using rituals to recover more efficiently and to better prepare for each upcoming point.

The performance consequences of instituting precise between-point rituals were dramatic. Imagine two players of relatively equal talent and fitness in the third hour of a match. One has been regularly recovering between points, while the other has not. Clearly, the second player will be far more physically fatigued. In turn, fatigue has a cascade effect. A tired player is more susceptible to negative emotions such as anger and frustration, which will likely push his heart rate still higher, and likely lead to muscular tension. Physical fatigue also makes it far more difficult to concentrate. The same phenomenon applies even for those of us who work in sedentary jobs. Imagine that you have been sitting for long and continuous hours at your desk, operating under very high pressure. Fatigue is a likely consequence, and so is susceptibility to negative emotions and to distraction, all of which ultimately undermine performance.

In tennis, Jim's research proved this in measurable ways. The more linear or unvarying players' heart rates became, the worse they tended to play and the more likely it was that they lost their matches. Too much energy expenditure without sufficient recovery caused their heart rates to become chronically elevated. Their performance was equally compromised when their heart rates remained chronically low—typically a sign that they were not committed enough or had given up the fight.

Even in a sport such as golf, which requires very little expenditure of physical energy, rituals that balance energy expenditure with recovery are critical. Jack Nicklaus was remarkable for his skill and consistency, but also for his remarkable ability to analyze the elements that contributed to his success:

Chapter 7: The Law Of Expectations

"Success is a journey, not a destination. The doing is often more important than the outcome."

- Anonymous

We questioned many of the most productive people we know where resources will meet the demands for success. They were not talking simply about physical energy, however about that hard to explain internal energy when pressed, nearly all placed internal energy above physical energy in terms of critical characteristics.

One standard error that individuals make is to believe that the only way to get more energy is to produce healthy lifestyle changes that focus on food and fitness. While that is one place we will cover that does drastically influence energy-- it is far from the only one. There are various types of energy and different sources of energy. Our daily way of life routines influences physical energy, however, there is likewise Emotional Energy, Production Energy, and Spiritual Energy, all of which can bring more zest and performance to your days.

I made these names based on the research that I have been doing. My working meaning of energy is "a sensation of individual power that allows us to continue favorable production or perusal of the need-to-do jobs in our lives."

Emotional Expectatins and "The Second Wind"

Have you ever been worn out and then pushed yourself to do something anyway? Maybe it was a dinner with a pal or going to a talk or lecture? Someplace inside that duration, the tiredness disappears and is changed by what we typically call "a second wind." That "2nd wind" is the energy that you are producing. It isn't something you need to wait on, and you can build that energy at any time as soon as you understand the actions that created it in the first place.

Finding emotional energy: This energy is originated from something that stimulates our emotions or our passions. We get new details or hear old information in a new way. Or perhaps we are around someone who imitates energy, and their love excites the energy within us.

All stimulus influences our energy one way or the other. Watch for an incentive that is affecting your energy levels adversely. Are your options inspiring and uplifting more energy or are they energy sappers?

Put it into Practice: To use Emotional Energy in your everyday life, you require to find what produces this energy for you. Develop a page in your notebook for noting your energy-producers. Here are a few that are on my list:

1. Check out favorable feedback or notes I have received from readers.

2. Have coffee, supper or lunch with somebody who I find motivating.

3. Check out a book that I discover motivational or inspiring--something that truly "speaks" to me.

4. Make sure I start my day of rest with positive psychological energy through my "Good Morning" routine.

5. Ask myself each morning, "Who do I want to be today?" and after that, stay personally accountable for being the very best "me" possible.

Physical Energy

Of course, we can't "talk" about energy without consisting of the physical aspect. Little modifications can make a massive distinction in your energy production.

I saw specialist Thomas Perls on CNN with Larry King and found his research quite fascinating and revealing. This free, online test is a fantastic method to look at the "spaces" in your life. Odds are where you fall brief on the health rating are many of the very same locations where you can improve and develop more energy.

Figuring out your individual quota can go a long method towards regulating your energy. Preferably you desire to get the same quantity of sleep each night to maintain optimal energy levels (you need to also go to bed at the very same time each night). Before starting, make sure you are not totally drained or tired out; otherwise, you are going to overcompensate on your sleep.

Sleep preparation: Make sure that you stop consuming at least 3 hours before going to sleep to permit everything to digest. Avoid caffeinated beverages after dinner. Make your space "sleep-friendly" by switching off the television and playing peaceful music.

The impacts of food: Since food is our primary energy source, it makes sense that excellent food will produce unique energy and bad choices will affect us adversely. Protein supplies more stable energy than carbohydrates which keep our body going like a rollercoaster!

Reduce starches and bread, rolls, bagels, pasta-- starches typically slow individuals down. Try going a week or 2 with minimal carbohydrates and see if this helps your energy level. You can perform the same experiment with caffeine.

Pop those vitamins: At a minimum take a tremendous daily vitamin. While you may not see a huge change, over long-term usage, this can assist prevent many of the conditions that sap energy.

Food patterns: Consider keeping a food journal to see how your energy changes with your food intake. Remember that eating to bit can be just as energy-sapping as consuming the wrong foods. Studies have revealed that those who eat breakfast have more energy.

Getting your body moving is one of the quickest methods to increase energy. Offer any exercise program about three weeks to begin offering you energy - the first three weeks can be tiring as we snap our bodies out of their comas! A current Prevention short article shared how doing only 10 minutes of LIGHT weightlifting repetitions caused a focus group to feel a 45% increase in their energy level.

Put it into Practice: It is essential to recognize that energy isn't a "one size fits all" formula. I motivate you to try out each idea, taking notice of how it affects your energy level. Pick one area to start with from the above list and schedule a "start date" on your calendar this coming week.

Efficient Energy

Among my objective group, individuals were stunned at her progress throughout her first week. While before the class she had felt not able to achieve the most basic tasks, she now discovered herself completing her objective-centered to-do lists-- and more! "How does that work?" she asked in a post to the assistance board.

When we repeatedly step forward, we propel ourselves forward even further. When we continually move backward, we dig a big hole.

To truly understand productive energy, think of a time when you were fatigued and then became inspired to do something. Well, you didn't consume anything or workout. Your attitude and productiveness rose - therefore elevating your efficiency and your energy.

Make a list ... and ensure to examine it two times: The very first action in structure efficient energy is to be focused on the right track. Have a clear list of what you want to achieve with available and clear timelines. Ensure to star three items for the day that will enable you to feel good about the day regardless of what bumps pop up in your course.

Get began early: Make sure to start your action list soon in the day to develop momentum. Consider registering in our Procrastination Primer class if you have problems with procrastination.

Recharge: To be efficient, you need to have balance and that indicates learning what you require to charge. Some people require a peaceful time each day; others just require a good night's rest. Discover what helps you charge and work that it into your to-do lists.

Forget revving your engine and go ... The fantastic feature of efficient energy is you don't need to prepare or invest a lot of time considering it. Frequently we over-think and would be far better off following the Nike motto. Press yourself over inaction and you'll discover that productive energy is all set and awaiting you whenever you require it.

Put it into Practice: Read through these four pointers and "star" which appears to talk to you the most to increase your Production Energy Arrange time to work in that location this month.

Spiritual Expectations

Spiritual energy can be considered "soul food." It isn't stress-filled or distressed motivation energy, however, calm and focused energy. Consider a time where you have experienced deep relaxation or a time where you have been moved by a preaching or spiritual reading/teaching. That centeredness is mental energy. The appeal of mental energy is that it is consistent and satisfying. It doesn't depend on "lows and highs" to keep recreating itself. It originates from listening instead of talking and "being present" instead of "trying to get someplace else." Since this is calm and peaceful energy and doesn't yell loudly for our attention, it is often the most ignored. Finding "peace" appears like an "extra" that several us do not have time to pursue. Within that peace, lies an ever-renewing source of energy. I would attempt to say that living without it is harmful-- and trying to live well without it, quite tricky.

Qualify spiritual practice: What does spiritual practice imply to you? It might be day-to-day time for reflection, meditation, or daily Bible research study or spiritual reading or prayer time. Think about the mental energy you've had in the past and if you include mental energy every day.

Make a pact: Make a pact with yourself not to starve yourself of this soul food. Remember this is peaceful energy that will not scream for your attention, so it is essential to nourish and dedicate to it.

Keep a spiritual journal: Make entries of your spiritual practice time and record what you find and learn. Use this as a source to return to once again and again to motivate continued spiritual advancement.

Journal: Journal about what life implies to you and the principle of "purpose." What is your function? At the end of your life, what do you wish to have completed here on earth and why? Use your journal to stay connected with your function. You can likewise try blogging about what "individual peace," means to you.

Generous a group: To remain on track with spiritual practice, think about a partner or group to touch base with regularly.

Chapter 8: Practicing the Art and Science of Goal Setting

"Chaos is a name for any order that produces confusion in our minds."

— *R. Buckminster Fuller*

The Power of Goal Setting

Just writing any goal down on a piece of paper won't make it happen. However, by taking the necessary steps (even small steps) towards your end goal, you will make it happen before you even know it. That is the power of goal setting.

But how do you take those steps? The answer, as we'll explore below, is the difference between wishing and planning.

Wishing Vs. Planning

Wishing you could do this and that won't make anything happen. Taking the steps to accomplish what you wish will help you achieve it. If you just wish to quit smoking, for example, but still carry a pack of cigarettes with you, what are the chances that you are going to quit?

Instead, if you make it your goal to stop smoking, and then make a plan and take the actions for it, your chances for quitting are higher, right?

It will look something like this:

-First, you make it your goal to stop smoking

-Then you list the reasons why you want to stop smoking:

- Save money
- Be healthier
- Smell better

-Then you list the small steps you have to take towards quitting:

- Going from one pack a day to one pack every three days
- Then one pack every seven days
- Then 10 days- making it 2 cigarettes a day
- Eventually quitting altogether
- Not having easy access to a pack
- Stay away from people that smoke for a while
- Get professional help if needed
- Acupuncture

You see, when you write down a goal with an action plan, it seems more possible, doesn't it?

If you are more of a visual person, creating your vision board will help you tremendously with setting goals and moving towards them. A vision board is a collage of images, words, or both that serves as a motivational tool to help you reach your goals.

Before you start putting together your vision board, you need to prioritize what is most important to you!

Ask yourself which areas of your life you want to improve. In what area do you need to focus now to make a positive change in your life? Is it your:

- Health
- Finances
- Marriage
- Career
- Personal Growth

After you have selected one area you are going to work on, the next step is to visualize your big picture.

You need to visualize the big picture in your head. For me, it was getting my degree. My big picture was walking up on stage during the commencement ceremony and getting my diploma.

When you are creating your vision board, try to think with the "end" in mind.

Ask yourself:

- How is achieving your goal going to change your life?

- Where do you see yourself one year from now?

- How does your life or lifestyle look now that you have accomplished your goal?

For example: Say you want to lose 25 lbs. That's your personal goal. That is a priority to you because you want to look better, feel better, and live a healthier lifestyle. You visualize how losing 25 lbs. is going to make you feel about yourself. How you are going to look? What kind of new clothes will you be wearing? What types of fun new activities will you be doing? How is it going to change your eating habits and lifestyle?

After you've spent some time thinking (and feeling!) about what your life will look like when you achieve your goal, it's time to create your vision board.

There are many ways to create a vision board, but my two favorites are:

- On actual poster board

- Drawn out in your notebook

Using a notebook is more convenient, easier, and faster. I start by putting the main category I want to work on in the middle of the page, then I add sub-categories all around the main one. Or, you can start by putting your goal on the middle and then writing a few bullet points that relate to achieving that goal.

Poster boards take more time but are also more fun to do. You start by writing down the main goal/category you want to accomplish in the middle of the board, then you add photos/images/and inspirational quotes/words all around it. Try to find photos that represent your goal. Your finished project should look like the same (or at least very similar) to the vision you had in your mind before you started creating your vision board.

After you create your vision board, make sure that you don't hide it in a closet, never to be seen again. You need to put it in a place where you can see it every single day. That can be by your bedroom where it is the first thing you see in the morning, or by your work desk where you can look at it throughout the day.

Setting goals

Is like putting

Your own dreams

On a vision board

With a due date on it.

Find Your Passion – Find Your Why

What do you love to do? You might already know what you want to achieve in life. You wrote down your big picture and your category, but now you have to ask yourself WHY?

The WHY it is going to be your motivating factor. The reason you are going to work every single day on the goals you've set for yourself.

Without the WHY, this whole process does not work because there is no one and nothing motivating you to work for it.

You go to work because you have bills to pay, so paying bills is your motivation for waking up, getting dressed, commuting, and doing a job that you might not even like every single day.

Going back to my goal of getting my degree, my motivating factor (or at least one of them) was that I wanted a better job.

I studied for the upcoming tests, I did my homework, I finished my assignments on time, all because in the back of my mind my WHY was always with me. I had enough motivation, and my WHY was important enough to keep me on track. With my WHY, I was able to push forward and not give up.

1. I want to help others set and achieve their goals, no matter where they are in life or what their background is. I want to help them be the best version of themselves. No matter who you are or where you are in life right now, there is always room for improvement. There is also enough room to make big goals and crush them. Maybe you always wanted to learn a new language, move to another country, save enough to take your family to Disneyland, lose 10 lbs., or whatever else your goal might be. It will be a great feeling knowing that I am able to help even one person reach what they want in life.

2. Help my favorite organization in Albania, "Fundjave Ndryshe ". I would be beyond thankful to have the opportunity to work with this organization. They work really hard to go all over Albania and help people with food, clothes, shelter, and whatever they need. They go to the most rural areas where sometimes there is no access to

clean water, give food and clothes to families, and even build homes for them. Having the opportunity to work with them will be amazing, both for people I am helping and for my own kids. My oldest boys, now 15 and 13, have been born and raised in the US. It will be such a worthwhile (and humbling) experience for them to get to help others and actually see that there is an entire world outside of what they have experienced in the US. I try as much as possible to travel with them; I want to show them other cultures and how we should accept and respect other people for who they are. However, it is a totally different scenario when you travel strictly for work, especially when you are helping others. I want to show my boys how rewarding it is when you give to others and help make their life a little bit easier.

3. I want the self-fulfillment of reaching my goal. Not too long ago, I wrote down "write a book" as one of my long-term goals. I don't really remember how the idea got to me or why it stuck, but I am so glad it did. As I wrote it down in my notes, I didn't think much about it. A few weeks later, I attended a conference in Orlando. After I registered and got my welcome bag that first day, I received a book by Chandler Bold called Published. I started reading it right away. I thought to myself: is this really a sign, or just pure coincidence?

I will never know for certain, but that book helped me go from writing a note to publishing my own book. OK, reading the book wasn't enough to do all that. The rest was up to me—taking the necessary steps toward those goals and following the path that I was supposed to lead to this book. My point is, just because I received a book it doesn't mean that I would read it or be interested in it. The same thing applies to my goals: just because I wrote down a goal doesn't make that goal happen. But persistence, discipline, and courage do.

To achieve a goal you need to:

Be Persistent - Do what you need to do every single day within the timeframe you set for your goal.

Have Self-Discipline - You cannot give up on a goal just because you find it to be too difficult, you get distracted, or because you are a procrastinator.

Have Courage – You must believe in yourself and your abilities.

Don't repeat the same old beliefs of I'm too old, I can't learn, I'm not strong enough, I'm not smart enough, I'm not young enough… These thoughts won't get you anywhere except the place you are in right now. And guess what? As long as your thinking is negative, there is no room for improvement or any positivity in your life. Even when all the doors of opportunity are open right in front of you, your mindset won't be able to see it.

Chapter 9: How To Defeat Procrastination And Disappointment

"People who succeed without effort have either great talent or a lot of luck."

- Jack Welch

In the journey to achieving more, goal-setting has always received lesser honor than it deserves; the concept is highly underrated among the elements that contribute to success in life. Even when it is the foundation of every successful business, career, achievement, just name it. Irrespective of what you chose as a profession or career, setting your goals right is crucial to your professional, finance, and personal productivity; even in your relationships, you need to set some goals properly. It's not everyone that takes goal-setting seriously. Some think it's like new year resolution; meanwhile, it's far beyond that. Efficient and effective goal-setting demands the goal-setter to be serious, calculative, and self-disciplined. Else, the goals may end up as ordinary goals without being achieved.

When setting your goals, you must get your objectives plainly defined. Clear the path you'll take to reach the goal - time-frame, needed resource versus available resources, and the sacrifice it may require. Due to the difference in human nature, different people take different routes to reach their goals, but then, some common criteria must be involved in your goal-setting techniques - SMART.

Making Your Goals SMART

When it comes to setting goals in the necessary facets of life, especially in the business world, the most recognized and endorsed strategy is SMART (Specific, Measurable, Achievable, Relevant, and Timed). The idea behind this system is to ensure that your goals are reasonable and concise. Some studies have proven that the application of this SMART mechanism can further save your precious time and make the whole process simpler. Let's get to see what it entails.

Specific: Every reasonable goal should be explicitly defined and highlighted for only its purpose. There must be a definite direction the goal focuses on. A clear plan of the expected end product must be sketched out unambiguously. Imagine a goal like "I want to attain a greater height next year." Greater height on what? It's rare and hard to achieve such radar-less goal. The author of The Success Principles, Jack Canfield, said in the same book, "Vague goals bring forth vague results." Therefore, in the process of setting SMART goals, you need to be as specific as possible.

Measurable: Another reason some goals are never fulfilled is because the goal-setters lose track of the set goals so easily. Why do they lose track of set goals? Simply because the goals were never made to be measurable. Any goal in life should have a way one can measure the progress from beginning until it's achieved, else, concentration can be lost easily. A quantifiable measurement is an attribute of every reasonable goal. That is not hard to deduce; there are several techniques you can generate to measure the progress of your goals. All you need is your intuition and readiness to do it.

Achievable: One thing is to set a goal while another thing is to set an attainable goal. It's often encouraged to set high goals, but it's highly advisable to make your goals feasible. A lot of people set unbelievable and almost impossible goals which they habitually don't reach. This will not but decrease your productive and demolish your morale to do more. What you know you can't chew, you shouldn't bite; neither should you chew what you can't swallow. You must be realistic with your goals so you will not seem like a brave-coward when you finally opt-out of the pursuit. Only the goals that are within your capacity are achievable, anything outside that is likely to waste your time. Don't plan on what you can't do at a particular moment.

Relevant: Human wants are different from needs. It is possible you really don't need what you want; therefore, what you need is more important than what you want. Don't make the mistake of setting goals only based on what you want without prioritizing what you need in the process of setting your goals. The major point here is that, let your goals be something that'll add value to you, especially at that time. Something that's relevant to you presently or in the nearest future. Don't waste your mental energy setting goals on how to relate with employees when you haven't even figured out the kind of organization you want to set up.

Timed: Similar to relevance, everything has its time of usefulness. A valuable goal set at the wrong time may be rendered useless because of its wrong timing. The perfect thing is to set the right goals at the right time with a reasonable deadline, of course. A meetable timeframe is a vital factor in the process of setting a long-term goal. It gives your subconscious mind to be more focused on accomplishing it before the set time. If critically viewed, the difference between you and the more productive people is their ability to set SMART goals. You think setting goals and achieving them is difficult to do? Review your self-discipline; you definitely need an amendment.

Actively Setting Goals

This is not among the SMART mechanism but can be wrapped around it. I wouldn't have touched this part, but many goal-setters don't know that actively setting goals is different from ordinarily setting the goals or passively setting the goals. When you actively set goals, it means that you set some goals in your mind, write them out, plan ways by which you can get them done, and then actively work towards achieving the goals. When you write your goals down, they have a more profound meaning to you than when they stay in your mind. Goals that are set to remain in mind are not goals until they have been written down and given meaning; until then, they are thoughts. When you wish to do something, don't just wish and leave it in your mind. Instead, write it out and then start planning towards how it would be achieved.

Time Management and Organization

This is another essential habit that you must cultivate if you are looking to improve on your productivity. Contrary to how simple it sounds; time management is a crucial habit that we must imbibe in both our professional lives and personal lives. Without it, self-discipline is questionable. Both the rich and the poor, the old and the young ones, we all got the same 24 hours per day - time, in fact, is a limited resource. To live a disciplined life, you must start with being organized. If you are a completely rough type, then you must build the habit of being organized over time. Slowly but surely, the more you try, the better you get. Start from organizing all those little things you scatter in your study at home or on your desk at your workplace. Pay maximum attention to those little things that seem trivial; they are the ones that affect our lives quite the most. When your physical environment is in a constant state of organization, your mind mirrors that, and it becomes calm, peaceful, and conducive. That's when you can vibrantly think of being more productive.

However, if your physical environment is always in a scattered state, you cannot find peace within yourself, too, because the mind would be restless. Time management, therefore, is sequential to the organization because they are like two peas in a pod. Once you are very organized, managing your time would pose no or little problem. Without the habit of time management, it becomes almost impossible to get anything done. When we can manage our time properly, we leave enough room to get those things that are actually important done. This means that we have enough room for those things that are likely to help us achieve our set goals. A person who cannot properly manage his/her time is a person who cannot learn to discipline himself/herself. Time management, organization, and self-discipline are like three kids from the same mother; they go hand-in-hand and collectively improve productivity.

Chapter 10: How to Increase Your Persuasiveness

"Never underestimate the power of a small group of committed people to change the world. Indeed, it is the only thing that ever has."

- Margaret Mead

There are many times when the human mind is pretty easy to influence, but it does take a certain set of skills to get people to stop and listen to you. Not everyone is good with influence and persuasion, though. They can talk all day and would not be able to convince others to do what they want. On the other hand, some could persuade anyone to do what they want, even if they had just met this person for the first time. Knowing how to work with these skills will make it easier for you to recognize a manipulator and be better prepared to avoid them if needed.

The first thing that we need to look at is what persuasion is. Persuasion is simply the process or action taken by a person or a group of people when they want to cause something to change. This could be concerning another human being and something that changes in their inner mental systems or their external behavior patterns.

The act of persuasion, when it is done properly, can sometimes create something new within the person, or it can just modify something already present in their minds. There are actually three different parts that come with the process of persuasion including:

- The communicator or other source of the persuasion
- The persuasive nature of the appeal
- The audience or the target person of the appeal

All three elements must be taken into consideration before you try to do any form of persuasion on your own. You can just look around at the people who are in your life, and you will probably be able to see some types of persuasion happening all over the place.

Experts say that people who are good leaders and who have good persuasion powers will utilize the following techniques to help them be successful:

- Exchanging
- Stating
- Legitimizing
- Logical persuasion
- Appealing to value
- Modeling
- Alliance building
- Consulting

- Socializing

- Appealing to a relationship

The above options are all positive ways that you can use persuasion to your advantage. Most people will be amenable to these happening. But on the other side, there are four negative tactics of persuasion that you can do as well. These would include options like manipulating, avoiding, intimidating, and threatening. These negative tactics will be easier for the target to recognize, which is why most manipulators will avoid using them if possible.

Now, you can use some of the tactics above, but according to psychologist Robert Cialdini, six major principles of persuasion can help you to get the results that you want without the target being able to notice what is going on. Let us take a look at these six weapons and how they can be effective.

The 6 Weapons of Influence

Reciprocity

The first principle of persuasion that you can use is known as reciprocity. This is based on the idea that when you offer something to someone, they will feel a bit indebted to you and will want to reciprocate it back. Humans are wired to be this way to survive. For the manipulator to use this option, they will make sure that they are doing some kind of favor for their target. Whether that is paying them some compliments, giving them a ride to work, helping out with a big project, or getting them out of trouble. Once the favor is done, the target will feel like they owe a debt to the manipulator. The manipulator will then be able to ask for something, and it will be really hard for the target to say no.

Commitment and Consistency

It is like humans to settle for what is already tried and tested in the mind. Most of us have a mental image of who we are and how things should be. And most people are not going to be willing to experiment, so they will keep on acting the way that they did in the past. So, to get them to work with this principle and do what you want, you first need to get them to commit to something. The steps that you would need to follow to get your target to do what you want through commitment and consistency includes:

• Start with something small. You can ask the target to do something small, something that is easier to manage the change before they start to integrate it more into their personality and get hooked on the habit.

• You can get the target to accept something publicly so that they will feel more obligated to see it through.

• Reward the target when they can stick to the course. Rewards will be able to help strengthen the interest of the target in the course of action that you want them to do.

Social Proof

This is another one that will rely on the human tendency, and it relies on the fact that people place a lot of value and trust in other people and in their opinions on things that we have not tried yet. This can be truer if the information comes from a close friend or a person who is perceived as the expert. It is impossible to try out everything in life, and having to rely on others can put us at a disadvantage. This means that we need to find a reliable source to help us get started. A manipulator may be able to get someone to do something by acting as a close friend or an expert. They are able to get the target to try out a course of action because they have positioned themselves as the one who knows the most about the situation or the action.

Likeability

We all know that it is easy to feel attracted to a certain set of people. This can extend to friends and family members as well. So, if you would like to get others to like you and be open to persuasion from you, you first need to figure out how to go from an acquaintance to a friend. This will work similarly to the reciprocity that we talked about earlier, but some of the basic steps that you will need to follow to make this work include:

- The attraction phase: You need to make sure that there is something about you that instantly draws the other person to you.

- Make yourself relatable: People are more likely to be drawn to you if you are relatable to them in some way. It is also easier to influence another person if they consider you, their friend.

- Communicate like a friend: Even if the two of you are not quite friends yet, you will be able to make use of the right communication skills so that the target will associate you as a friend.

- Make it look like you are both in the same groups and that you are fighting for the same causes: This can make it easier to establish a rapport with them.

Authority

If you want to make sure that you can influence another person, then you need to dress and act the part. This means that you should wear clothes, as well as accessories, that will help you look like you are the one in command. Some of the ways that you can do this include:

- Wear clothes that are befitting to what people will perceive an authoritative figure would wear.

- When you communicate with the target, you need to do so in a commanding fashion.

- Make sure that you can use the lexicon and the language of experts in that field.

When you can position yourself as the authority figure, people will look to you for the answers that they need. It does not matter how well they know you or not. You will have a great opportunity to influence them the way that you want them to behave.

Scarcity

The last weapon that you can use for persuasion is known as scarcity. Humans like the idea of being exclusive and are drawn to anything that they are not necessarily able to find anywhere else. When you make something exclusive, you have a chance of making it appear more valuable. People are also going to become fearful when something they desire starts to disappear. This whole idea is part of the supply and demand principle. If you have something abundant, then it will be perceived as having a lower value and cheap. But if it is rare, then it must have a higher value and be more expensive.

This can work for human beings and products in the same way. Some things that you should keep in mind when you want to use the scarcity principle with persuasion include:

• Always imply that the thing you are offering is not going to be available to the target anywhere else.

• If you can, it is a good idea to implement a countdown timer on what you are offering. This gives a physical indicator to the target that what you are offering is truly going to disappear.

• You should never go back on the stipulations that you said in the beginning. You need to make sure that the target knows that what you offered is scarce, or this method is not going to work very well.

Chapter 11: Why You Should Learn The Principles And Rules Of A High-Performance Person; How To Learn The Art And Science Of Goal Setting.

"If you don't set goals, you can't regret not reaching them."

- Yogi Berra

There's a commonly cited Ivy League study that supposedly shows writing down goals helps us achieve them. The problem is it's phony. And when people discover this, they sometimes think the benefits of writing down our goals are fake too.3 But no.

Professor Gail Matthews of Dominican University of California conducted her own study not long ago and confirmed the power of writing down our goals. She recruited 267 entrepreneurs, executives, artists, healthcare professionals, educators, attorneys, and other professionals from several different countries. She divided them into five groups and tracked them over several weeks. Matthews discovered, among other things, the mere act of writing one's goals boosted achievement by 42 percent.4 these gels with my own experience and that of people I coach.

Committing your goals to writing is not the end game. But it is foundational for success for at least five reasons. First, it forces you to clarify what you want. Imagine setting out on a trip with no particular destination in mind. How do you pack? What roads do you take? How do you know when you have arrived? Instead, you start by picking a destination. Clarity is a precondition for writing. (Ask any author suffering writer's block; they can't write because they're unsure what they're trying to say.)

Second, writing down goals helps you overcome resistance. When we go to the trouble of formulating and recording our goals, we're doing more than dreaming. We're also engaging our intellect. We're processing, self-checking, and analyzing. Every meaningful intention, dream, or goal encounters resistance. From the moment you set a goal, you will begin to feel it. But this emotional and intellectual engagement helps us identify deeply with our goals and forge resolve around our desires. I'll focus on this later in Step 4.

Third, it motivates you to take action. Writing your goals down is only the beginning. Articulating your intention is important, but it is not enough. You must execute your goals. You have to take action. I have found that writing down my goals and reviewing them regularly provokes me to take the next most important action.

Fourth, it filters other opportunities. The more successful you become, the more you will be deluged with opportunities.

Chapter 12: Proper Living is the Key To High Performance

"If you want to make the world a better place, start by making your world a better place."

- Kurt Vonnegut

High-Performance Habits of Top Leaders

The following habits are habits that high performing top leaders have. If you want to become a high performing top leader, you need to do it on purpose. These habits are going to help you become a top-performing leader so that you can be the best leader that you can be while leading the best team efforts possible.

Seek Clarity in Everything

With everything that you do in life, you should always seek out clarity. Although you are not always going to find clarity, seeking clarity will help you find your true path and ensure that you are always as educated as possible. Clarity helps you stay focused on what you are aiming for because you are always looking for the information that you need to help you stay focused on what is important, thus making it easier to sift through what classifies as a distraction so that you can let it be.

When you are seeking clarity, also seek out the opportunity to review your own behaviors and characteristics to ensure that you are behaving in alignment with what truly matters to you. Clarity is, after all, all about priorities and knowing what matters and what doesn't.

To help you seek clarity in a more focused and direct way, pay attention to these four things: skills, self, service, and social. What skills are going to help you get to where you want to go in life? How do you want to be able to describe yourself? What services do you want to provide? How do you want to behave in social situations? Get clear on who you are and regularly revisit these questions to ensure that you are always focused on what you are truly going for and clear as to what you bring to the table.

Generate Energy for Yourself

An incredible number of people lose energy rapidly and have no idea how to regain energy once it is lost. The infamous "mid-afternoon energy drop" is something that many of us experience and most have no idea how to get out of the slump once it hits. Of course: high-performing leaders do not have time for energy slumps because they have the stuff to get done, so they are always looking for ways to energize themselves and keep themselves going. In order to stay high performing without wiping yourself out or compromising on your energy, you should stay as focused as possible on what needs to get done. Distractions are a huge reason why people find themselves getting drained: because they are not focused on their priorities and so they end up wasting energy.

When you take a break in between activities, give yourself a quick moment to close your eyes or meditate so that you have a short mental break before you transition to your next activity. This way, your brain does not feel like it is "going" all the time, allowing it to fully rest in between periods of activity. Through doing this, you can improve your odds of staying energized enough to continue going all day long. This is because you are recharging yourself between activities, rather than further draining yourself.

Make It Necessary

If you do not have a strong reason for why you are getting something done, you are going to suffer big time struggling to get yourself focused and ready to take action. One of the biggest reasons why people procrastinate is because they have not made something necessary enough for them to actually consider it a priority. When you start working toward producing high-performance results, you need to start raising the bar on your way.

A great way to attach a necessity to what needs to get done is to assign a person to your reasoning. Find out who you need to be acting on behalf of so that you can make them proud or help them in some significant way, and then make them your way. A great question to ask yourself is: "Who needs me doing my best today?" Then do whatever you are doing for them. This way, you have a strong and compelling reason for why you are going after the results that you are heading for.

Increase Your Productivity

If you want to become a high performing leader, you need to learn how to increase your productivity. Your productivity is a direct review of how well you are keeping yourself together and mastering both your mindset and your action. If you need to increase your productivity more, you can do so by focusing on what actually matters. Instead of trying to produce top quality results in everything, including the things that do not really matter to your bottom line, focus on producing top quality results in those that matter. Then, scrap everything else.

This is not just concerning your products, sales numbers, and work performance, either. Although those are important for being a leader, you need to look broad spectrum. In your whole life, focus on what matters and do your best to devote your time to what you actually need to be doing, rather than everything else. When you can effectively prioritize, you will find yourself making strides toward the successful completion of your goals.

Develop Your Influence

A leader does not lead through commands and demands because they know that this is unlikely to produce results. Since they are results-oriented, they know that being overly bossy and trying to demand things from people is generally a waste of time. Instead, they develop their influence so that people are inspired by them and aspire to be like them. This way, they can really develop productivity in their team because they are modeling the very behaviors that their team members are aspiring to produce within themselves.

You can develop your influence by helping people learn how to think. When you teach people how to see things from a different perspective, how to approach things from a different angle, and how to create their own opinions, you teach them to think. When you can positively impact someone's thoughts, you become influential in their lives because you effectively teach them how to access more of their brainpower and become a better person.

Demonstrate Courage Daily

Courage is a powerful strength to have, and every high performing leader is courageous. In fact, high performing leaders demonstrate courage on a daily basis as a way to push themselves beyond their own limits and into something far greater. Each day you should seek to find something that is an act of courage, and then you should aim to act on it so that you can demonstrate courage.

When possible, let your impressionable team see you courageously leading so that when they aspire to be like you, they are doing so in a positive way.

Create Rituals for Yourself

Finally, if you really want to become high performing, it is not enough for you to know what comes with becoming a high performing leader. You need to put the effort in to become high performing. You need to be willing to set rituals for yourself that encourage you to engage in these habits, as well as ones like positive thinking, and you need to follow those rituals every single day.

You can create as many rituals as you want. The key is that you make a ritual that you can consistently practice anytime the right trigger is pulled. For example, say when you feel fearful, you choose to have a ritual that helps you build courage so that you can demonstrate courage. Your ritual might consist of repeating a mantra, recalling a person who gives you courage, choosing a person or people that you are doing it for, and then taking the first step. Customize your ritual process to fit your needs and choose one that really helps you amplify the power of your mind so that you can get to where you want or need to go effortlessly.

How to Coach Your Team on These Habits

Naturally, having your team behaving in alignment with these habits can be powerful, too. If you want to have the best team possible that is all moving toward the same goals and producing the same high-performance results; you need to know how to coach your team to have these qualities as well. Below are five steps to help you begin to coach your team to be high performers while behaving like a high-performance coach yourself!

Teach Them How to Be Energetic

Just like you, your team is likely going to have the same experience of an energy crash in the early afternoon. If left unresolved, this could lead to your entire team having a major drop in productivity later in the day. Once in a while, productivity drops like this are nothing to worry about. However, if your entire team, or even just most of your team, is experiencing this productivity drop at the same time every day, this can lead to a lot of lost productivity in a minimal amount of time. To avoid this, you have to teach your team how to keep their energy up so that they can keep going all day long.

A great way to help keep your team productive is to educate them on the power of their mind and to encourage regular brain breaks throughout the day. Showing your team how to set their devices aside, sit down in quiet, and let their brains have a pause is a great opportunity to educate them on how they can avoid the mid-afternoon crash every day. You can even make the brain breaks a regular thing with your team by offering them an additional 5-minute break every so often to do nothing and let their minds reset. Although they are going to be on break longer than they may have been previously, they will be coming back from those breaks rejuvenated and ready to work once again. As a result, they will have significantly stronger productivity following the break, which means that more will get done. In the end, the added breaks will pay off as long as your team members are using them for the right reason.

Encourage them to Find Inspiration

A great way to coach your team to seek inspiration is to educate them on where courage comes from. Teach your team to pick a person that they are showing up for, beyond themselves, and to use that person as their inspiration to be brave and to get their work done on a regular basis.

Chapter 13: How To Get Motivated

"Motivation is like a fire. If you do not tend it, it will go out."

- Abraham Lincoln

Double your money

Put money aside for projects and opportunities that come your way. Pay off your bad debt and put money aside. Save it somewhere you can access it within a month. This money will help you seize your opportunity and it will also act as an emergency fund to help you avoid getting into bad debt in times of emergency. It becomes very difficult to react quickly and seize your opportunity if you don't money put aside and if you are in debt. The money you put aside will also help you double your money.

You double your money by buying products that are under-priced and selling them back at market price or above market price. You can flip a house. Buy a house that is below its market value and sell it back at market price or above market price and make a profit. I will write a book about property flipping which will explain everything you need to know about that for now let us stick to the point. The point is that there are many things that you can buy below market price and sell them at a higher price. You must keep your head up and look for desperate sellers who want quick money because of their financial crisis and that's your opportunity to double your money. The model is simple: buy low, sell high. You can do it with anything. It can be property, vehicles, clothes, etc. The fourth industrial revolution is bringing vast opportunities in the information technology field, you can double your money with that.

Another way to double your money is through government tenders. You can be creative and find other ways to double your money. The point is doubling your money becomes possible and easier if you have money put aside. This is known as saving your money, however, most people don't like the idea of saving money because they usually associate it with being the middle class that's why I call it putting money aside for projects. Everything in life needs money, directly or indirectly. Get a job, save money and then find something that you can sell to a million people. This money will help you take action when an opportunity becomes available and it will help you stay out of bad debt. Bad debt can ruin your life and it is one of the top reasons why people don't become rich. Use the money that you save as an emergency fund. If an emergency comes then you use the money you saved instead of taking loans. If you take out a loan, you will spend months paying it back which will prevent you from taking your opportunity. And worse, what if another emergency comes while you are still paying off your loan, then you have to take another loan. Like they say, when it rains it pours. When you have an emergency fund set up, then focus on growing your money to become rich. If you don't have money to close your bad debt and save, get a job. Getting a job is super easy I will show you how.

Educate Yourself

I have already covered this, but I just want to stress it enough. I want to give you the perspective and the strategy. We all know that wealthy people read over 50 books a year. The is a direct relationship between reading and being rich. Let me put it in another way, you won't get rich if you don't read. Now, let's kill two birds with one stone. Register for a course and read the books that you will get a certificate for. This will guarantee that when you finish your course, will you have both the certificate and the knowledge. Use the certificate to grow your career and the knowledge to make money.

Spend less than you earn

No matter how much you earn, spend less than you earn then invest the rest of the money or save it or use it to study. Remember studying is considered as growing your business. Information is that powerful. Spend only 10% of what you make on fun activities. Yes, this includes cheating expenses. That's why I prefer not to cheat. Yes, I will write a book about dating. I was given a gift to put things into perspective and that's exactly what I am going to do. Back to spending. Spend less than you make. Only use 60% of what you earn on essentials.

Fix your mentality

Getting rich is not only possible but it is easy. You just have to do all the right things and that includes having the right mentality. There are two ways to get the right mentality, you can either hang around rich people or read a lot of books. I do both. Remember, you and I still need to redefine reading.

Do the math

Simple math really, we have already done this. If you sell your skills to a million people at one dollar each then you have one million dollars, before tax. I will talk about tax. If you are an employee and you sell your skills to a large organization, then you get a million-dollar salary. That's why growth is the key to being rich. Remember the rich keep getting richer. This means if you do it once, you will keep growing rich provided you keep growing your IQ.

Add value in people's lives

The amount of money you make is equivalent in one way or the other to how many people you reach out to. You must sell your product, skill, or services to as many people as possible and the easiest way to do that is to create a product, offer a service or sell a skill that offers value to people's lives. If you make a product and sell a million units of that product, then you have a million dollars. If you have a skill and you sell it to a million people, then you have a million dollars. The only way to get a million people to buy what you are selling is if it adds value to their life. Soccer players are selling their skills to millions of fans for entertainment. The richest people in the world are using their knowledge to make products and they sell them to millions of people because their products add value.

Be Grateful

The more you work hard and smart the more opportunities will come your way. People will help you, you will attract a positive vibe. Be grateful and work even harder and smarter. Just remember the darkest hour, is the hour before dawn.

Rules of Money Management

- Track your finances daily.
- Don't spend more than you earn.
- Generate passive income.
- Never stop reading.
- Put your employment benefits to good use.
- Pay your bills on time.
- Invest in education.
- Stick to your budget.

High-Performance Person

Divide your day into quadrants

During planning, you should divide your day into 4 quadrants. If you are awake for 16 hours per day, each quadrant should contain four hours. By planning your day this way, you will be able to put tasks into blocks of time. You will also be aware of how productive you have been by checking your output at the end of each quadrant.

We usually spend the first quadrant preparing for the day ahead; this is where your morning ritual takes place. If you live far from your workplace, part of this time will also be used for commuting. Part of this quadrant will also be spent for the start of your workday. You should take on your most essential tasks in this quadrant.

The second and the third quadrants are where the rest of the workday happens. It is when we are most awake and productive. The last quadrant is usually spent with the family over dinner (or personal leisure time if you live alone). If you have a unique project, you may also use this part of your day to work on that.

Divide each quadrant into 15-minute chunks

If the 4-hour quadrants do not work for you, you may also choose to divide your working period into 15-minute chunks. A 15-minute period is long enough for you to start something and short enough for you to start and finish most of your shorter activities. Let's say you plan to work for an hour. You set your alarm to go off every 15 minutes. Every time the alarm goes off, you check your mood. If you still feel like working, you should continue until the alarm clock goes off again.

If you feel like you are tired when the alarm clock goes off, you should take a break. Your break time should only be 15 minutes long. The next time the alarm sounds, you should get back to work. It works better for people who get bored quickly.

This method is also beneficial if you often neglect essential tasks because you think there is not enough time. We often neglect tasks that we classify as "important but not urgent."

Manage your energy

Your will power to work weakens as your energy level goes down. By the time you start your final quadrant, your energy level is at its lowest. This is the reason why most people no longer have the will power to work at home.

Now that you know how your energy level depletes during the day, you should try to readjust your schedule so that the most critical tasks are done at the time of day when your mind is most awake. If you are working on a personal project outside of work, for example, you should put it in your schedule early in the morning right after your morning routine. If there is too much commotion at home, you can also do your project in your office right before you start the workday.

Motivate yourself for work right before a new quadrant starts

The advantage of dividing your day into parts is that you get to restart your day for each division. Let's say you are already tired after your day's second quadrant. Most people will give up on the workday. They will spend the rest of the workday with half the energy level they had in the morning. When doing their tasks, their attention is on time rather than on their tasks.

It is not that they do not have the energy; they lack the motivation to do their work. Over time, this becomes a habit. They habitually decrease their energy level on the third quadrant of their day. For most people, the pattern develops because they forget their reason for working at this point of their day. Even if they were extremely productive in the morning, they still end up providing the output of mediocre quality.

If you usually enter the same mental state in the later parts of your day, you should find ways to re-motivate yourself right before you start a new quadrant. By doing so, you remind yourself of the things that motivate you to work.

From your records, you should categorize your activities. For a working mother, for example, the activities may be divided into these categories:

- Family
- Work

- Personal time
- Socialization

Some of us are guilty of spending too much time in one category. We usually over-do something that feels good. The goal of categorizing your tasks is to become aware of how you balance your time. When you are aware that you are spending too much time in one aspect of your life, you will be able to modify your behavior.

Analyze and re-strategize

In this activity, you should examine your weekly planning notebooks. It would help if you compared your plans to what happened. If things did not go as planned, you should not be too hard on yourself. Instead of blaming yourself or others, you should focus on what you can do to prevent deviations from the plan in the future.

It would help if you looked for time-wasting events that occur regularly. You should identify the causes of these time management problems and try to look for solutions. If a particular strategy does not work for you, you should look for other ways to deal with your time management problems. After all, dealing with the same issue may not always require you to stick to just one approach.

Look for positive changes and make them your habits

As you examine your logbook and your planner, you should look for areas where you have improved. You should see if there are changes that you can make that would further enhance your performance. It would help if you also made habits out of these positive changes. By developing time-conserving habits, you will be able to make positive changes permanent.

Aim for efficiency

The ultimate goal is to continually look for strategies that will improve your efficiency at work and home. You will only reach maximum effectiveness if you are no longer distracted by time wasters. You will need the self-discipline to resist the urge to give these time wasters your attention. However, if you successfully ignore these distractions, you will reach your goals sooner, and you will have more time for your other priorities in life.

Enjoying life isn't necessarily about having free time and being great at everything. It's about disciplining yourself and making it a point to improve on your weak points. Some people are content with the way they are.

To enjoy your life as being motivated and productive, you must learn to put the procrastination habit on the shelf and leave it there to rot. It's not easy. If you are used to putting aside tasks until you feel like doing them, making yourself do them right away is going to feel uncomfortable for a while. Once you get into the habit, you will find that you enjoy being productive and laugh at yourself for the times when you would procrastinate it.

Not only will you enjoy being productive and managing your time well, but others will notice the difference in you. You will find that you're more relaxed and not feel pressured by large amounts of work. It will all come in time. You're not going to be able to change years of habits overnight.

Just remember, procrastination leads to stress, and stress leads to a less enjoyable life. Just because you're intimidated by the list of tasks before you, don't make the situation worse by procrastinating them. Take some of the tips that I've mentioned and make yourself face your struggle head-on.

Once you've found a balance between time management and focus, you will notice that your tendency to procrastinate has gone way down. Great job! Continue to build healthy time management habits so that you won't fall into the trap of procrastination again.

There are a thousand and one ways that each of us starts our morning. Although some of us start our morning much later, all of us have a specific time that we consider morning. Productivity is usually very high in the mornings; hence, it is vital that you accomplish as much as possible during this time. It makes a morning routine a very fundamental part of effective time management as well as productivity.

High-Performance Person

Mornings are the perfect time to be creative, exercise as well as have some 'me time'. Additionally, science has indicated that a person's willpower is most influential in the morning. It means that if we want to be productive, we must take advantage of these and perform tasks that will be more difficult as the hour's pass. How you spend your morning is also a precursor to how your day shall progress. A calm and productive morning will yield calmness and productivity throughout the day, while a hectic and frantic morning ritual will generate much of discord during the day.

What do you aspire to do in life? Where do you want to be? How are you going to get there? These are some of the most pressing questions that we ask ourselves throughout our lives. Our inability or unwillingness to answer these profound questions can cause us to remain in a state of discontent. While I can share how I have tackled and addressed those same exact questions, I know that this book is not about me, but it is about you. I want to help you recognize your true worth, walk in your greatness, and learn how to think your way up. You must learn, develop, create, and then share your own secrets of success and how you have learned to think your way up.

In life, we have two choices regarding excuses. We can either uncover the blueprints of our lives or pursue our purpose; or we can create excuses that push us away from living a life of greatness. Every one of us has a purpose and an awaiting destination. We can create excuses that block us or use those excuses as a bridge that will help us reach our destination. The journey is there and the route you choose to take is solely up to you. What bridge are you willing to take today?

Success story of Soichiro Honda

In 1930, when Japan was taken away by the Great Depression, Soichiro Honda was still in school. In 1937, he started developing 'piston rings' in a small workshop.

He wanted to sell the idea to Toyota and worked extremely hard for it. After working day and night, Honda was finally able to complete his piston rings and took a working sample to Toyota for examination.

Toyota rejected his piston rings. Reason: it did not meet their quality standards!

He went back to school where other engineers made fun of him, but he didn't give up. For two more years, Honda worked relentlessly on the design and refinement of his piston rings.

He submitted them again to Toyota and this time won a contract!

Now, he needed a factory to supply materials to Toyota. Unfortunately, Japan was gearing for war at the time, and resources were in short supply. He couldn't find enough cement to build his factory, so he developed a new process to create cement himself!

High-Performance Person

Soon the factory was constructed and was ready to begin production. But fate had other ideas. His factory was bombed twice, and steel became unavailable at the same time.

It really tested the resolve of Soichiro Honda. But he still didn't quit, only changed his approach.

He collected gasoline cans discarded by US fighters and started using them as new raw materials in his newly rebuilt manufacturing process.

As things started to look better, an earthquake leveled his factory yet again. Any ordinary person would have given up at that point. But he persisted.

After the war, there was a huge shortage of gasoline in Japan. People began to either walk or ride their bicycle to their destination. Honda saw an opportunity and attached a tiny engine to his bicycle.

His neighbors saw it and requested one for themselves. Honda tried to meet the demands, but he couldn't, as resources like material and money were lacking.

Instead of being disappointed, he looked for possible solutions.

He wrote an inspiring letter to 18,000 bicycle shop owners to help him revitalize Japan by innovation. Out of which 5,000 responded and forwarded whatever resources they could to him.

Then he began developing small bicycle engines. Initial ones were bulky and didn't work. After continuous refinement and development, however, he created a small engine "the super club" which became quite successful.

Soon, he began exporting his bicycle engines to Europe and America, establishing the brand of Honda overseas.

Later, when the world was moving towards small cars, Honda saw an opportunity and started manufacturing small cars. His expertise in creating small engines paid dividends and Honda cars became a runaway success.

Today, the Honda Corporation has more than 175,000 employees on multiple continents and became one of the largest automobile companies in the world.

All because of Soichiro Honda's willingness to learn take action, change approach and a firm commitment to his dream...

Conclusion

To make meaningful and consistent progress along that spiral, we need to consider one other aspect of renewal as it applies to the unique human endowment that directs this upward movement—our conscience. In the words of Madame de Staël, "The voice of conscience is so delicate that it is easy to stifle it: but it is also so clear that it is impossible to mistake it."

Conscience is the endowment that senses our congruence or disparity with correct principles and lifts us toward them—when it's in shape.

Just as the education of nerve and sinew is vital to the excellent athlete and education of the mind is vital to the scholar, education of the conscience is vital to the truly proactive, highly effective person. Training and educating the conscience, however, requires even greater concentration, more balanced discipline, more consistently honest living. It requires regular feasting on inspiring literature, thinking noble thoughts and, above all, living in harmony with its still small voice.

Just as junk food and lack of exercise can ruin an athlete's condition, those things that are obscene, crude, or pornographic can breed an inner darkness that numbs our higher sensibilities and substitutes the social conscience of "Will I be found out?" for the natural or divine conscience of "What is right and wrong?"

Steve Meyer

In the words of Dag Hammarskjöld,

You cannot play with the animal in you without becoming wholly animal, play with falsehood without forfeiting your right to truth, play with cruelty without losing your sensitivity of mind. He who wants to keep his garden tidy doesn't reserve a plot for weeds.

Once we are self-aware, we must choose purposes and principles to live by; otherwise the vacuum will be filled, and we will lose our self-awareness and become like groveling animals who live primarily for survival and propagation. People who exist on that level aren't living; they are "being lived." They are reacting, unaware of the unique endowments that lie dormant and undeveloped within.

Thank You!

Hope you've enjoyed your reading experience.

So I'd like to thank you for supporting me and reading until the very end.

It will mean a lot to me and support me in creating high-quality books, for you in the future.

Thanks once again:

Warmly yours,

Steve V. Meyer

Steve Meyer

Download Your Free Gift

Before you go any further, why not pick up a gift from us to you?

GROWTH PRINCIPLES

If you're willing to learn and transform yourself in all the right areas,

then success is definitely for you.

So, to find out how you can do that, let's get reading.

Scan the barcode to get it before it expires!

Feel free to continue your journey with us, where you will find new resources, tools, blogs, and advanced notice of new books at...

www.booksandsummaries.com

www.ingramcontent.com/pod-product-compliance
Lightning Source LLC
Chambersburg PA
CBHW050255120526
44590CB00016B/2354